Reflection

The Azrieli Series of Holocaust Survivor Memoirs: Published Titles

ENGLISH TITLES

Judy Abrams, *Tenuous Threads/* Eva Felsenburg Marx, *One of the Lucky Ones*
Amek Adler, *Six Lost Years*
Ferenc Andai, *In the Hour of Fate and Danger*
Molly Applebaum, *Buried Words: The Diary of Molly Applebaum*
Claire Baum, *The Hidden Package*
Bronia and Joseph Beker, *Joy Runs Deeper*
Tibor Benyovits, *Unsung Heroes*
Pinchas Eliyahu Blitt, *A Promise of Sweet Tea*
Max Bornstein, *If Home Is Not Here*
Sonia Caplan, *Passport to Reprieve*
Felicia Carmelly, *Across the Rivers of Memory*
Ben Carniol, *Hide and Seek: In Pursuit of Justice*
Stefan A. Carter, *A Symphony of Remembrance*
Judy Cohen, *A Cry in Unison*
Tommy Dick, *Getting Out Alive*
Marie Doduck, *A Childhood Unspoken*
Marian Domanski, *Fleeing from the Hunter*
Anita Ekstein, *Always Remember Who You Are*
Margalith Esterhuizen, *A Light in the Clouds*
Leslie Fazekas, *In Dreams Together: The Diary of Leslie Fazekas*
John Freund, *Spring's End*
Susan Garfield, *Too Many Goodbyes: The Diaries of Susan Garfield*
Myrna Goldenberg (Editor), *Before All Memory Is Lost: Women's Voices from the Holocaust*
René Goldman, *A Childhood Adrift*
Elly Gotz, *Flights of Spirit*
Ibolya Grossman and Andy Réti, *Stronger Together*
Pinchas Gutter, *Memories in Focus*
Anna Molnár Hegedűs, *As the Lilacs Bloomed*
Rabbi Pinchas Hirschprung, *The Vale of Tears*
Bronia Jablon, *A Part of Me*
Helena Jockel, *We Sang in Hushed Voices*
Moishe Kantorowitz, *Lament*
Margit Kassai, *Between the Lines: The Diary of Margit Kassai*
Jack Klajman, *The Smallest Hope*
Eddie Klein, *Inside the Walls*
Michael Kutz, *If, By Miracle*
Ferenc Laczó (Editor), *Confronting Devastation: Memoirs of Holocaust Survivors from Hungary*
Eva Lang, David Korn and Fishel Philip Goldig, *At Great Risk: Memoirs of Rescue during the Holocaust*
Nate Leipciger, *The Weight of Freedom*
Alex Levin, *Under the Yellow & Red Stars*
Rachel Lisogurski and Chana Broder, *Daring to Hope*
Fred Mann, *A Drastic Turn of Destiny*
Michael Mason, *A Name Unbroken*
Leslie Meisels with Eva Meisels, *Suddenly the Shadow Fell*
Leslie Mezei, *A Tapestry of Survival*
Muguette Myers, *Where Courage Lives*
David Newman, *Hope's Reprise*
Arthur Ney, *W Hour*
Felix Opatowski, *Gatehouse to Hell*
Malka Pischanitskaya, *A Mother to My Mother*
Marguerite Élias Quddus, *In Hiding*
Maya Rakitova, *Behind the Red Curtain*
Henia Reinhartz, *Bits and Pieces*
Betty Rich, *Little Girl Lost*
Paul-Henri Rips, *E/96: Fate Undecided*
Margrit Rosenberg Stenge, *Silent Refuge*
Steve Rotschild, *Traces of What Was*
Judith Rubinstein, *Dignity Endures*
Martha Salcudean, *In Search of Light*

Kitty Salsberg and Ellen Foster, *Never Far Apart*
Morris Schnitzer, *Escape from the Edge*
Joseph Schwarzberg, *Dangerous Measures*
Zuzana Sermer, *Survival Kit*
Rachel Shtibel, *The Violin*/ Adam Shtibel, *A Child's Testimony*
Maxwell Smart, *Chaos to Canvas*
Gerta Solan, *My Heart Is At Ease*
Zsuzsanna Fischer Spiro, *In Fragile Moments*/ Eva Shainblum, *The Last Time*
George Stern, *Vanished Boyhood*
Willie Sterner, *The Shadows Behind Me*
Ann Szedlecki, *Album of My Life*
William Tannenzapf, *Memories from the Abyss*/ Renate Krakauer, *But I Had a Happy Childhood*
Elsa Thon, *If Only It Were Fiction*
Agnes Tomasov, *From Generation to Generation*
Joseph Tomasov, *From Loss to Liberation*
Leslie Vertes, *Alone in the Storm*
Anka Voticky, *Knocking on Every Door*
Sam Weisberg, *Carry the Torch*/ Johnny Jablon, *A Lasting Legacy*

TITRES FRANÇAIS

Judy Abrams, *Retenue par un fil*/ Eva Felsenburg Marx, *Une question de chance*
Amek Adler, *Six années volées*
Molly Applebaum, *Les Mots enfouis : Le Journal de Molly Applebaum*
Claire Baum, *Le Colis caché*
Bronia et Joseph Beker, *Plus forts que le malheur*
Max Bornstein, *Citoyen de nulle part*
Salomon Buch, *Un serment à la vie*
Tommy Dick, *Objectif : survivre*
Marie Doduck, *L'Enfant du silence*
Marian Domanski, *Traqué*
John Freund, *La Fin du printemps*
Myrna Goldenberg (Éditrice), *Un combat singulier : Femmes dans la tourmente de l'Holocauste*
René Goldman, *Une enfance à la dérive*
Pinchas Gutter, *Dans la chambre noire*
Anna Molnár Hegedűs, *Pendant la saison des lilas*
Helena Jockel, *Nous chantions en sourdine*
Michael Kutz, *Si, par miracle*
Eva Lang, Fishel Philip Goldig, David Korn, *Un si grand péril : mémoires de sauvetage durant l'Holocauste*
Nate Leipciger, *Le Poids de la liberté*
Alex Levin, *Étoile jaune, étoile rouge*
Fred Mann, *Un terrible revers de fortune*
Michael Mason, *Au fil d'un nom*
Leslie Meisels, *Soudain, les ténèbres*
Muguette Myers, *Les Lieux du courage*
Arthur Ney, *L'Heure W*
Felix Opatowski, *L'Antichambre de l'enfer*
Marguerite Élias Quddus, *Cachée*
Henia Reinhartz, *Fragments de ma vie*
Betty Rich, *Seule au monde*
Paul-Henri Rips, *Matricule E/96*
Margrit Rosenberg Stenge, *Le Refuge du silence*
Steve Rotschild, *Sur les traces du passé*
Kitty Salsberg et Ellen Foster, *Unies dans l'épreuve*
Morris Schnitzer, *Sur la corde raide*
Joseph Schwarzberg, *Sur les sentiers de la guerre*
Zuzana Sermer, *Trousse de survie*
Rachel Shtibel, *Le Violon*/ Adam Shtibel, *Témoignage d'un enfant*
George Stern, *Une jeunesse perdue*
Willie Sterner, *Les Ombres du passé*
Ann Szedlecki, *L'Album de ma vie*
William Tannenzapf, *Souvenirs de l'abîme*/ Renate Krakauer, *Le Bonheur de l'innocence*
Elsa Thon, *Que renaisse demain*
Agnes Tomasov, *De génération en génération*
Leslie Vertes, *Seul dans la tourmente*
Anka Voticky, *Frapper à toutes les portes*
Sam Weisberg, *Passeur de mémoire*/ Johnny Jablon, *Souvenez-vous*

Reflection

Hedy Bohm

WITH THE ASSISTANCE OF
Myrna Riback

FIRST EDITION

The Azrieli Foundation · azrielifoundation.org

The Holocaust Survivor Memoirs Program
Publisher, Naomi Azrieli · Director, Jody Spiegel · Managing Editor, Arielle Berger
Cover and book design by Gareth Lind
Edited by Devora Levin and Arielle Berger
Endpaper maps by Martin Gilbert. Interior map by Merritt Cartographic.
Back cover photo by Justine Apple Photography, courtesy of Friends of Simon Wiesenthal. Background image: iStock.com/Danijela Racic. Digital copies of the images on pages 122 (1 and 3), 131 (1), 132 (1), 133 (1), 134 (2) have been provided courtesy of Crestwood Oral History Project.

Library and Archives Canada Cataloguing in Publication

Reflection / Hedy Bohm ; with the assistance of Myrna Riback.
Bohm, Hedy, 1928– author. | Riback, Myrna, author. | Azrieli Foundation, publisher.
First edition. | Azrieli series of Holocaust survivor memoirs ; 18
Includes index.
Canadiana (print) 20250318423 | Canadiana (ebook) 20250318512
ISBN 9781998880300 (softcover) | ISBN 9781998880317 (EPUB)
ISBN 9781998880324 (PDF)

LCSH: Bohm, Hedy, 1928– | LCSH: Holocaust, Jewish (1939–1945) — Romania — Oradea — Personal narratives. | LCSH: Jews—Romania—Oradea— Biography. LCSH: Jews—Hungary—Biography. | LCSH: Jews—Romania—Transylvania — Biography. | LCSH: Holocaust survivors —Romania — Oradea —Biography. LCSH: Holocaust survivors — Canada — Biography. | LCGFT: Autobiographies.

LCC DS135.R72 073 2026 | DDC 940.53/18094984—DC23

PRINTED IN CANADA

Contents

Series Preface: In Their Own Words

In telling these stories, the writers have liberated themselves. For so many years we did not speak about it, even when we became free people living in a free society. Now, when at last we are writing about what happened to us in this dark period of history, knowing that our stories will be read and live on, it is possible for us to feel truly free. These unique historical documents put a face on what was lost, and allow readers to grasp the enormity of what happened to six million Jews—one story at a time.
David J. Azrieli, C.M., C.Q., M.Arch
Holocaust survivor and founder, The Azrieli Foundation

SINCE THE END of World War II, approximately 40,000 Jewish Holocaust survivors have immigrated to Canada. Who they are, where they came from, what they experienced and how they built new lives for themselves and their families are important parts of our Canadian heritage. The Azrieli Foundation's Holocaust Survivor Memoirs Program was established in 2005 to preserve and share the memoirs written by those who survived the twentieth-century Nazi genocide of the Jews of Europe and later made their way to Canada. The memoirs encourage readers to engage thoughtfully and critically with the complexities of the Holocaust and to create meaningful connections with the lives of survivors.

Millions of individual stories are lost to us forever. By preserving the stories written by survivors and making them widely available to a broad audience, the Azrieli Foundation's Holocaust Survivor Memoirs Program seeks to sustain the memory of all those who perished at the hands of hatred, abetted by indifference and apathy. The personal accounts of those who survived against all odds are as different as the people who wrote them, but all demonstrate the courage, strength, wit and luck that it took to prevail and survive in such terrible adversity. The memoirs are also moving tributes to people—strangers and friends—who risked their lives to help others, and who, through acts of kindness and decency in the darkest of moments, frequently helped the persecuted maintain faith in humanity and courage to endure. These accounts offer inspiration to all, as does the survivors' desire to share their experiences so that new generations can learn from them.

The Holocaust Survivor Memoirs Program collects, archives and publishes select survivor memoirs and makes the print editions available free of charge to educational institutions and Holocaust-education programs across Canada. They are also available for sale online to the general public. All revenues to the Azrieli Foundation from the sales of the Azrieli Series of Holocaust Survivor Memoirs go toward the publishing and educational work of the memoirs program.

The Azrieli Foundation would like to express appreciation to the following people for their invaluable efforts in producing this book: Maryanne Reed and Alison Strobel.

Editorial Note

THIS MEMOIR WAS written about a time when territories in Eastern Europe were frequently changing hands. As borders shifted, names of cities, towns and villages changed, as did official languages. In the period Hedy writes about, the region where she lived was alternately part of Romania, Hungary and Nazi Germany. Though it was part of Romania during her youth, there was large population of Hungarian speakers in the region, and Hedy refers to the places of her childhood by their Hungarian names. However, she uses the Romanian name of the city in which she grew up, Oradea, by which it is currently known, rather than Nagyvárad, its Hungarian name.

Foreign-language words and historical terms that may be unclear without additional context have been added to the glossary beginning on page 143.

Introduction

> In April 1944, my mother sewed a yellow Star of David on my coat. That's when I felt marked for the first time. Still, I had no inkling of what was to come. I couldn't understand why we were being singled out. I wondered what we had done — my parents and the other Jews — to warrant it. Even then, my parents didn't explain anything to me, and I was confused as to why I couldn't go to school or why we had to wear the star. I don't remember if I asked questions. If I did, there were no answers provided. I suppose my parents were trying to protect me from fear and the brutal reality of what the rumours suggested.

THIS IS HOW Hedy Bohm, born in 1928 in the city of Oradea, remembers her first encounter with antisemitism. Aged just fifteen, she was thrust into a world of escalating danger, her "ideal life of parents, home and school" abruptly disrupted by persecution, displacement and unimaginable loss when Hungary was occupied by Nazi Germany in 1944. *Reflection* is her account of surviving the Holocaust as a lone adolescent girl: confused, frightened and largely "oblivious" of the genocidal violence that engulfed her life until it was already unfolding. Written eighty years after Hedy's liberation, her memoir shines a light on the particular sufferings of young victims coming of age during the Holocaust, violently torn from the safety of their home lives and families, in some cases with little understanding of the genocidal processes to which they were subject.

Hedy's naïveté — a recurring theme throughout her memoir — stemmed in part from her sheltered upbringing. Her parents, Erzsebet (née Breuer) and Ignac Klein, chose not to tell her about the Nazis' persecution and murder of Jews elsewhere in Europe. Doing so, they perhaps believed, would shield her from fear of the family's targeting by Nazi antisemitism — a word Hedy encountered for the first time in 1944 — and enable her to lead a worry-free childhood. Like many assimilated Hungarian Jews, her parents also felt the Nazi regime posed little threat to them, especially at such a late stage in the war. After all, the Kleins were not a particularly observant Jewish family; they spoke Hungarian rather than Yiddish at home, attended synagogue infrequently and considered themselves "Hungarian city people" first and Jews second. What was more, Hedy's father had fought for Hungary during World War I and therefore believed his family would be protected from danger by the Hungarian government. This combination of familial silence and social assimilation meant that Hedy was wholly unprepared for the shattering of her life and the horrifying conditions she would soon be forced to endure when the Nazi occupation of Hungary began in March 1944.

Often protecting her from the abject horror she would suffer and bolstering her will to live *in extremis*, Hedy's naïveté would go on to shape her experiences for the remainder of the war. When the family was forced into the Oradea ghetto in May 1944, for example, she remembers that both she and her parents remained unafraid, certain that they would be put to work on farms or in factories until the war's end. Later that same month, when the Kleins were deported from the ghetto to Auschwitz-Birkenau in crowded freight cars, Hedy worried little about their destination, not only because the presence of her parents offered her a sense of security, but because she was ignorant of the mass murder of Jews in Poland. In the camp, at which the family arrived on a sunny day in early June 1944, Hedy remembers feeling, above all else, intense confusion. She had no concept of where she was or what purpose the camp served, and she was unaware of the gas chambers in which her parents would soon be murdered. When she was separated from her mother upon arrival at Auschwitz-Birkenau, Hedy never suspected that her mother had been selected for death. Instead, she was sure that they had been parted temporarily and would reunite once the war was over. This illusion sustained her, driving her "ability to improvise, to go on, to survive" while imprisoned in Auschwitz-Birkenau and, later, in the Fallersleben and Salzwedel concentration camps in Germany.

Hedy's story—and indeed, the naïveté that characterizes it—cannot be fully understood without placing it in the context of Hungarian Jewish history and the particular trajectory of the Holocaust in Hungary. Her birthplace, Oradea—known as Nagyvárad in Hungarian and Grosswardein in German—was in the region of Transylvania, a region whose political and national status has shifted repeatedly throughout history. After World War I and the disintegration of the Austro-Hungarian Empire, the Treaty of Trianon (1920) severely diminished Hungary's size, giving large parts of its territory—and population—to Romania and Czechoslovakia. Northern Transylvania, including Oradea, was transferred from Hungary to Romania. For many ethnic Hungarians, this shift in national borders was a deep wound. In 1940, however, the Second Vienna Award, brokered by Nazi Germany and Fascist Italy, returned Northern Transylvania to Hungary. The re-annexation was welcomed by many Hungarians, including schoolchildren in Oradea like Hedy, who appreciated the change in their language of education from Romanian to Hungarian, with which most of them were more familiar.

Oradea was also home to a long-standing Jewish community, with its first synagogues and communal Jewish schools built in the early 1800s. From the mid-nineteenth century onwards, Hungary's Jewish population became increasingly divided between two main groups: the Orthodox, who were typically based in the rural northeast, and modern Conservative Jews, who embraced greater degrees of acculturation and secularism. Hedy's family fell firmly into the latter category. The Kleins were, she writes, "very different from the religious communities in the northeast. We lit Shabbat candles and went to synagogue maybe three times a year: on Rosh Hashanah, Yom Kippur and maybe once more. And that was it as far as our Jewishness went." Jewish life in Oradea reflected these broader national trends. In the early twentieth century, Jewish liberalism flourished in the city, and many Jewish residents found success in public and professional life. Some opened factories or established businesses, while others worked in respected roles as doctors, lawyers, merchants and, like Hedy's father, craftsmen. Meanwhile, in the rural northwestern fringes of Oradea, many Yiddish-speaking Jews lived in poverty and held fast to traditional ways of life.

The religious divide in Hungary's Jewish community had repercussions for the Klein family. Hedy was never told much about her parents' lives before her birth—something she would come to regret—but she does describe her maternal grandparents' desire for her mother to marry an Orthodox Jewish man. Instead, her mother chose Ignac Klein. Rather than continuing her education, which her family could not afford for her to do, Hedy's mother worked in the delicatessen, which was bought for her by her family, until her marriage to Ignac. Reflecting on her mother's thwarted ambitions to pursue a career as a doctor, Hedy recalls: "My mother was a terribly disappointed, unhappy woman."

Perhaps owing to her mother's despondency, Hedy's relationship with her was, throughout her childhood, a complex one. On the one hand, Hedy relied upon and spent a great deal of time with her mother in the family home, and she recounts some early memories in which her mother was especially affectionate and caring. On the other hand, Hedy remembers that her mother was mostly cool and distant; she showed very little interest in Hedy and avoided interacting with her when they were together. Hedy's father, by contrast, was affectionate and playful. But he worked long hours as a relatively low-earning cabinetmaker and was frequently absent from the house. As an only child with a cold, withdrawn mother and a father often busy working, Hedy's formative years were largely solitary. She spent most of her time escaping into fantasy via the novels of Hungarian authors or expressing herself through painting and playing the piano—something she struggled to do in words as a shy and timid child. She only became properly socialized with other children once she started school, but even then, she remained inward-looking: "I was usually happy being alone."

This was the peaceful—if imperfect—life Hedy was living in Oradea when it was re-annexed to Hungary as part of the country's efforts to reclaim the territories it had lost after World War I. Shortly after it was awarded Northern Transylvania in September 1940, Hungary became a formal partner in the Axis alliance with Nazi Germany. This was a strategic move, for the Hungarian government viewed the Axis powers, especially Germany, as essential to regaining and maintaining its lost territories and restoring the nation's borders.

These events intensified existent antisemitic sentiment in Hungary, which had been growing throughout Hedy's childhood. As early as 1938, when Hedy was just ten years old, the Hungarian government, under the leadership of Admiral Miklós Horthy, had fostered friendly diplomatic relations with Nazi Germany based on the alignment of their world views. Under its own initiative, Hungary enacted anti-Jewish laws, beginning in 1938 with a law that restricted Jewish participation in certain industries and limited the number of Jews in many professions to 20 per cent. Subsequent Jewish laws passed between 1939 and 1941 introduced racial criteria for defining Jewishness, barred intermarriage between Jews and non-Jews, and expelled Jews from cultural, social, economic and political life in Hungary. The fascist and virulently antisemitic Arrow Cross Party, fashioned after the Nazi Party, was also formed in 1939. By 1940, Transylvania was back under Hungarian control and many Hungarian Jews living there had become the targets of Hungarian antisemitism. In addition, "politically unreliable" men, as well as all Hungarian Jewish men of military age, were conscripted for forced labour service by the Hungarian government.

For Hedy, however, life carried on as normal. She did not feel the effects of anti-Jewish laws, and her father was exempt from forced labour after sustaining serious injuries in an accident the previous year. In fact, in the absence of competition from other Jewish cabinetmakers in Oradea as a result of conscription, Hedy's father's business boomed, and the Kleins' financial situation improved.

By early 1944, more than four years into the war, the Holocaust had already claimed the lives of millions of Jews across German-occupied Europe. Yet, Hungary's Jewish population — numbering over 800,000 — had not yet been subjected to ghettoization and mass deportation. This was because in 1942 Horthy had resisted pressure from the Nazi-German government to deport its Jews to German-controlled territory, concerned that the expulsion of its sizable Jewish population would have a significant impact on Hungary's economy. It is therefore no surprise that in 1942, when Hedy's auntie Margit travelled from Bratislava to urge the Kleins to leave the country after the arrest of her husband and children in the collaborationist Slovak Republic, they did not heed her warnings. For the time being, at least, Hungarian Jews, though discriminated against by anti-Jewish legislation and forced labour service, did not share the fate of those living under direct Nazi occupation. As a result, Hungary was considered somewhat of a safe haven for Jews. It received thousands of Jewish refugees, like Hedy's auntie Margit, who desperately fled the Nazis' systematic mass murder of Jews in neighbouring countries.

However, in March 1944, Nazi Germany launched Operation Margarethe and occupied Hungary. Quick to comply with Nazi demands, Horthy installed a pro-German, right-wing antisemitic puppet government in Hungary under Döme Sztójay. The new government moved rapidly: antisemitic decrees intensified, Jewish property was seized, Jewish movement was restricted and the wearing of the yellow Star of David was mandated from April 5th for all Jews over the age of six. Hedy remembers these changes vividly. Her school was shut down, her radio confiscated and her family marked as Jews through the forced wearing of the yellow badge on their clothing. This latter decree, she recalls, legitimized the violent antisemitism of non-Jewish Hungarians: "The star became an open invitation for anyone who wanted to abuse

Jews without repercussions, rather with the encouragement of all those around."

Hungarian and German authorities began establishing ghettos across Hungary in the spring and summer of 1944. In them, Jews would be concentrated prior to their deportation for mass murder. Oradea's main ghetto, centred around the city's Orthodox synagogue, was the second largest in Hungary; at its peak, it contained 27,000 Jewish inhabitants. Three of those inhabitants were the Kleins, who were forced from their home and into the ghetto by Hungarian gendarmes in May. There, they lived under crowded and inhumane conditions, and faced the viciousness of the Nazi collaborators, who "surpassed even the Germans in their cruelty." Within a month, however, the Kleins would find themselves forcibly displaced once again.

By mid-May, Hungarian gendarmes, in coordination with Adolf Eichmann's SS deportation experts, had begun liquidating the Hungarian ghettos. Within two months, over 437,000 Hungarian Jews were deported to killing centres in Nazi-occupied Poland. Most were sent to Auschwitz-Birkenau. Over late May and early June, the main Oradea ghetto and its smaller counterpart—included eight thousand Jews—were evacuated in nine transports, one of which contained the Klein family. Hedy's description of the deportation—three days and nights in a freight car with no food, water or space to lie down—is detailed and harrowing. And yet, even in recounting this traumatic experience, her most enduring pain stems from what she *doesn't* remember: "I don't remember, in all those three days and nights, one word spoken between me and my mother and father. If there was, I wish I could remember what was said. But I don't." What Hedy, in her naïveté, could not have known then, was that these would be the last days she would ever spend with her parents.

Parted from her mother and father upon arrival at the camp, Hedy, like many other young survivors of the Holocaust, recalls the intense pain of this separation. For Hedy, it was the last image of her mother, walking among a group of women, children and the elderly to their deaths in the gas chambers, that stayed with her above any other. She writes:

> That's when I shouted after my mother. I was being ripped apart inside. She heard my scream and turned around, and we looked at each other. I don't know what I expected, maybe that she would come and get me and tell the Nazi soldier not to stop me, to let me go and join her. Whatever I expected was not what happened. We just looked at each other, my mother and me, without a word, she turned and kept walking away, and I was left standing there.

With hindsight, Hedy reflects in her memoir on the agony that her mother must have experienced as she was torn away from her only child, and questions whether she knew that she was walking to her death. Hedy, however, did not know. Only sixteen years old and ignorant of camp operations, she recalls asking herself in bewilderment, "Where were they going, and why was my mother going without me?" Despite the complexity of their relationship prior to the war, Hedy felt safest when she was with her mother; belief that she would return to that maternal care alone enabled Hedy to persist in the frightening and unfamiliar world of Birkenau. She remembers: "I believed that the only thing that would prevent me from being with my mother at the end of the war was if I didn't survive it."

For three months in Auschwitz-Birkenau, Hedy suffered the brutal conditions of the BIIc women's camp. A combination of resourcefulness, determination and the enduring memory of her mother helped her to survive. In Auschwitz-Birkenau, for example, a trip to one of its infirmaries was often considered a death sentence for sick prisoners, who received inadequate treatment and lived in squalid conditions on smaller food rations than other prisoners. When she fell ill with diarrhea, therefore, Hedy felt instinctively that she must avoid the hospital at all cost. She remembered her mother's home remedy—charcoal—and searched the camp for burned wood to chew on to settle her stomach. She bathed daily with cold water, forced herself to consume the revolting soup because "my mother would want me to drink it," and focused her efforts on remaining physically and mentally strong. She did so alone, never losing hope that if she could only survive, she would one day see her mother again. Unlike many other accounts by female survivors that emphasize mutual support and life-saving bonds among female prisoners, Hedy's story of the concentration camp is striking in its depiction of solitude. "I was alone, day after day, week after week," she remembers. "Being alone, I only concentrated on my own needs."

After three lonely months in the camp, Hedy visited her aunt and two cousins, who were housed far away in another barracks. On one of her infrequent visits, Hedy was selected with them, and the four were deported via cattle car to Fallersleben, a satellite camp of Neuengamme concentration camp in Germany. There, she worked as a forced labourer in an arms factory until she was transported with her aunt and cousins to Salzwedel, where she was liberated by the US Army in April 1945.

Liberation, however, did not bring an end to Hedy's struggles, nor deliver the meeting with her mother that she had long anticipated. On the day of liberation, she was informed by her aunt and cousins that her mother had been murdered in Auschwitz-Birkenau's gas chambers upon their arrival. She recalls: "I didn't want to live when I found out. I felt I couldn't. I knew I would be alone in the world now, and that was a terrible reality that I could not face." Indeed, Hedy would battle loneliness and isolation for much of her adult life thereafter.

Returning to Oradea, Hedy was taken in by her aunt and uncle. She secured a job as an apprentice in a photographic studio and in 1947, at the age of nineteen, she married Imre Bohm at the Orthodox synagogue in Oradea. Convinced that Romania—to which Oradea once again belonged in accordance with the Treaty of Paris (1947)—would soon become a dictatorship under the communist regime, Imre persuaded Hedy that it was best for them to leave the country before it became a challenging place to live. Together, they made the difficult decision to emigrate.

In August 1948, with the help of a friend, the couple pretended to be cousins in order to join a group of orphaned Jewish children bound for Canada as part of the Canadian War Orphans Project. The program, lobbied by the Canadian Jewish Congress, was designed to bring a thousand orphaned Jewish children to Canada to help them rebuild their lives in the war's aftermath. The Canadian Jewish Congress and the wider Canadian Jewish community took full responsibility for their care, housing them upon arrival and providing foster homes where necessary. After Hedy and Imre landed at Pier 21 in Halifax, Nova Scotia, they boarded a train to Toronto to be temporarily housed.

But life in Canada was not easy for Hedy. She and Imre moved from apartment to apartment, and between them they made barely enough money to survive. Eventually, in 1954, the couple opened a modest shoe shop and were successful enough to live a moderately comfortable life. Now financially stable, Hedy and Imre had two children. Hedy, however, bore the brunt of the domestic responsibilities: raising two children, managing the household, paying the bills and helping run the store, with little support from her husband. Here, as throughout the war, Hedy had to rely primarily on her own tenacity to survive, and to craft a meaningful life for herself in the wake of trauma and inconceivable loss.

In Canada, too, Hedy once again found herself terribly lonely. Orphaned and far from Hungary and the loving relatives—aunts, uncles and cousins—who had survived the Holocaust, she felt like a stranger to all around her in Toronto. To make matters worse, Canadian society had little interest in the difficult pasts of Jewish refugees. Repressing her wartime experiences thus became vital to the continuation of her life in Canada: "I had to go on ignoring, burying and not talking about my experiences if I wanted to survive." Ultimately, Hedy felt that both assimilation in this new and unfamiliar country, and her ability to function in the present, rested on her silence about the unimaginable struggles she had been forced to endure in the war years.

In the early 2000s, however, Hedy found her voice. Like many other survivors of the Holocaust, she felt a duty to speak for those who did not survive and could not speak for themselves. With the support of her daughter, Vicky, Hedy learned to control her emotions enough to share her testimony publicly. She soon began working with the

Holocaust Education Centre in Toronto, telling her story to non-Jewish Canadian schoolchildren to raise awareness of the Holocaust. She even returned to Auschwitz for the March of the Living and found the strength to testify at war crimes trials in Germany. In this way, Hedy not only discovered her life's purpose, but redefined herself. No longer the reticent child who could not speak up for herself, nor the newly arrived immigrant whose painful past had to be buried in the pursuit of love, belonging and stability in Canada, Hedy devoted herself to using her voice to keep the memory of the Holocaust alive. By doing so, she aimed not only to honour those who did not survive, but to encourage kindness and compassion in her listeners. That, she hoped, would be her legacy.

Although written decades after the events it recounts, Hedy's memoir offers a powerful glimpse into what it meant to be caught in the web of genocide during the Holocaust. It captures the abrupt rupture of girlhood, the agony of familial loss and the enduring impact of traumatic experience in the Holocaust. Unlike many other memoirs by female Holocaust survivors, which often foreground support networks and emotional solidarity between women, Hedy's story is defined by solitude and quiet resilience. Her account deepens our understanding of the diverse ways that Jewish girls came of age under Nazi rule, and the ways they lived and made sense of their persecution, deportation and imprisonment. It is also testimony to the afterlife of trauma and the manner in which it continued to shape survivors' lives and identities long after the war had ended.

Fundamentally, Hedy's account is more than just a story of survival. It is a moving window into the particular experiences of one war orphan who, despite loss and lasting loneliness, rediscovered her voice and committed to using it to make "the world just a teensy little bit better." *Reflection* is a heartfelt call to action for us to do the same.

Dr. Rosie Ramsden
Modern German History, Manchester Metropolitan University
2025

Legend
Borders in 1938
Annexed/occupied by Germany in 1938
Annexed/occupied by Germany in 1939
Occupied by Germany in 1941
Acquired by Hungary in 1938–1941
Occupied by Germany in 1944
Elbe
Bergen-Belsen
Salzwedel
Fallersleben
BERLIN
GERMANY
Vistula
WARSAW
POLAND
Oder
PRAGUE
Protectorate of Bohemia and Moravia 1939–1945
Auschwitz-Birkenau
CZECHOSLOVAKIA
Slovakia 1939–1945
Danube
VIENNA
Bratislava
AUSTRIA
BUDAPEST
Oradea (Nagyvárad)
HUNGARY
Körös
Transylvania
ITALY
ROMANIA
0 100 200 km
YUGOSLAVIA
© 2025 – The Azrieli Foundation

Let this telling of my story stand in the place of flowers on the nonexistent graves of the millions of Jews whose stories were wiped out by evil before they could be lived and told.

1

A Quiet Life

I WAS BORN on May 11, 1928, in Oradea, a thriving city in the region of Transylvania, which was part of Romania at that time. I was an only child, and I had a safe and quiet life. Nothing foreshadowed or prepared me, even in the slightest way, for the unbelievable hell that was about to be unleashed upon me, my family and all those I knew and loved.

My father was the warm one in my family, the soft one. He was not much of an authority figure, and he was always loving and caring, even though the times we interacted or played together were few and far between. Once, when I was around four or five, he came home from work early. He was wearing a heavy coat, and he asked me to come over to him. I went to kiss him, and he told me he had a present for me. He told me to put my hand in his pocket where the present was, and when I reached in, I felt something alive and warm moving. It startled me, and I pulled my hand out. My father laughed and took a little bird out of his pocket and gave it to me. It was a tiny speckled brownish bird, and he had a cage for it too. I was delighted.

The next morning when I woke up, I rushed to the kitchen to see my bird. But the cage was empty, and my mother told me that the bird had flown away. I was sad but I accepted it. I just hoped the bird would be happy. Of course, now I realize that my mother had let the bird go because she didn't want to keep a caged bird in the house. She was a practical woman of strong convictions.

One of my favourite memories with my father is of when we were still living in our first apartment, so I would have been less than six years old. One summer evening, as it was getting dark, we were coming home from a visit to my maternal grandmother, who lived not too far away from us in Oradea. Our house was about a thirty-minute walk from hers, and we were halfway home when I got tired and started to complain. My father picked me up and put me on his shoulders, and I hugged him and hung on tight. I was really happy in that moment. I felt so safe, on top of the world as I looked at everything around us. I felt loved and secure.

The playfulness that there was in my father was missing in my mother, but I still had a nice relationship with her. I depended on her totally because she was the only one around. My mother was matter of fact and not emotional or physical at all, not given to hugging and kissing like my father. She didn't teach me much, and I don't remember ever having a conversation with her or her telling me a story or anything about herself or my father. For that matter, I don't remember her ever being interested in what interested me. She had little patience or interest in me. Well, maybe she did have an interest in me, but she didn't know how to show it.

Even though my mother was not very tender or affectionate, I do have a few early memories of times when she was more loving and caring than usual. One of my earliest memories is of a time when I was with my mother in the kitchen, where she was preparing to iron clothes. I must have been about two years old, and I was sitting on the potty and watching her. She had a huge piece of wood, a thick paddle of sorts, about three feet long, with a handle that made it look like a weapon. After she sprinkled the sheets or shirts with water and rolled them up, she would hit them with this paddle. To keep me occupied, she had allowed me to look at her beloved women's magazine, *Tolnai Világlapja* (Tolnai World Page), which she got once a week. There was a two-page spread showing pictures of a laboratory in which there were instruments and beakers of different shapes and sizes, full of liquids with lamps underneath them heating them up. There was also a researcher in a white coat. I was fascinated by the different shapes of the beakers—thin ones and wide ones, tall and small ones—and I imagined what it would be like to be there in that laboratory. It is a happy memory.

Another early memory of my mother is of a time when I was sick. She had covered the lamp near my crib with a pinkish cloth so that the harsh light wouldn't disturb my sleep and sat at the table near me, reading. I wanted to hear the words she was reading and begged her to read out loud. But she said the novel was not suitable for children. I begged and begged her until she relented and started reading. I didn't understand a word of what she was saying, but that wasn't important. She was reading to me. Hearing her voice was soothing and reassuring.

I must have had influenza or a bad cold and was pretty ill. I couldn't swallow medication. I suppose my mother was at her wit's end trying to get medication into me, but I just wouldn't cooperate. She tried putting it in anything she could think of, crushed up in cream of wheat or with milk, but when I tasted it, I would throw up or spit it out. I remember her leaning over my crib and looking at me. I looked into her eyes and thought, *Oh, she does love me.*

2

Memories of Family

I DIDN'T GET to spend much time with my father because he was working constantly to make a living for us. He left home before seven in the morning, when I woke up, and my mother and I hardly ever had dinner with him since he usually worked till eight or nine in the evening, or even ten sometimes, six days a week. My father was a maker of fine cabinetry and had a shop where he made beautiful custom furniture for the wealthy people of the city. He had six or seven people working for him. His customers could choose whatever wood and veneer (walnut, oak or cherry) they wanted, as well as the style of cabinets from numerous albums he had. I used to visit him in his shop when I was a child and I particularly remember the massive presses he had there. Veneers were glued to pieces of wood, which were then put into the press, tightened and left to dry and become shaped. When that was done, the finished pieces would be polished for weeks to get the right patina.

Although he was a wonderful cabinetmaker, my father was not a good bookkeeper or businessman. My uncle Feri often tried to help him with his bookkeeping, but it didn't seem to make a difference. My father couldn't figure out how long it would take for the work to be finished or how to charge enough. My mother always had to worry about where the rent money was coming from, which didn't add to her happiness or satisfaction. She didn't work because there were few jobs for women in those days. I had over thirty classmates at school, and only two of them had mothers who worked. My girlfriend Hedy's mother worked in a cleaning shop, giving out or receiving items to clean or dye, and the other working mother was a cosmetician. All the other mothers stayed home with the children.

Every household in those days depended on being able to go to the market every day. There were no refrigerators and only the better off had iceboxes. We did not. From early spring to late fall, my mother went to the market daily to get whatever local produce was in season, and once or twice a week, meat or poultry. That was all that was available. Imports were a luxury, and we had none in our home.

I didn't like to eat in general, but I particularly didn't like most meat. My parents tried to encourage me to eat meat, just a little bit, and when my mother insisted, I ate it. Luckily, we had meat only on the weekends and she made other foods that I did like. Beef was available but was too expensive. We ate mostly chicken or duck, or goose in the winter. These were preferred because of the fat, which was rendered and used in cooking. My mother didn't like the idea of using oil, and most Jewish people used chicken and goose fat for cooking. Nothing was wasted. My mother would buy a whole goose, and it was an entire procedure preparing the breast and the legs for smoking. She would pound the legs with a mallet to flatten them and then rub them very thoroughly with garlic and Hungarian paprika, lots of it. She had two or three wooden sticks with pointy ends that she used for the specific purpose of poking through the meat under the skin to keep it stretched before she took it to a special place that smoked the meat. When it came back, it was delicious. I really loved smoked goose.

For dinner we often had homemade noodles, sweet with walnuts and poppy seeds and sugar, or savoury with cottage cheese and sour cream. I loved both of those noodle dishes. My mother also made sautéed cabbage with square noodles, a very Hungarian dish, or baked potato casserole with eggs, butter and sour cream layered in it. There was also goulash, or stews, cooked in the oven, and baked desserts with yeast, like babkas with chocolate, and cheese Danishes, which I could have lived on. We had a chicory substitute for coffee, but I didn't like it. When my mother wasn't looking, I would pour mine down the drain.

My mother made soups too. We often had chicken soup with noodles, and in the summer, we had cold fruit soups of all kinds, made from apples, cherries, plums or peaches. There was also cold bean soup served with dollops of sour cream. These soups were my favourite meals.

But there were some soups my mother made that I did not like, especially sweet and sour egg soup, which turned my stomach. She would make me that soup for lunch before I started going to school, but I couldn't eat it even though my mother told me I had to. She wouldn't let me leave the table until I did. One time, I was still sitting at the table with the soup in front of me when my father came home from work late in the evening. My mother told him I had been disobedient and wouldn't eat my dinner so he had to spank me. He had never spanked me before or laid a hand on me, so when he took me into the bedroom and made me lie down on the bed and spanked my bottom, I was heartbroken. Not that it really hurt; he didn't spank me hard. To make matters worse, I then had to go back to the table and eat the soup.

I think that for my mother it wasn't so much about my eating the soup as it was about her believing it was important to teach me obedience and discipline and for children to do what their parents told them to do. I suppose she was strict with me because she was afraid of what might happen to me since her first child had died.

Luckily, once I started school, I didn't have to eat that egg soup anymore for lunch. I brought sandwiches with me: two slices of bread with butter and jam, or a bit of goose fat and slices of smoked goose leg or thigh on bread—my favourite in the winter.

On Fridays mornings, my mother baked cheese or plum Danishes for Shabbat. Though we had little, she would bring baked goods to her unmarried cousins who lived alone. On Friday nights, my mother and I often had our Shabbat dinner with Auntie Ilus (Ilona) because my father wasn't home yet and Ilus's husband, Feri, was away on business. We'd light candles and have a simple meal. My mother would make her special appetizer called false fish. It was made out of minced chicken breast boiled with carrots, potatoes, onions and spices. We ate it cold and it was delicious.

I don't know how or when my mother and father, Erzsebet (Elizabeth) Breuer and Ignac Klein, met, or if it was love that brought them together or if their marriage was an arranged one. I know very little about my parents' lives because they never told me and I was not encouraged to ask. What I wouldn't give for just an hour with them again, to ask them questions about their early lives, their growing up years, their hopes and dreams, and what happened before they became my parents. I can only make up stories in my head from the little I know.

My father's parents came from small villages near Oradea. My mother's parents, Berta (neé Tischler) and David Breuer, came from Oradea. My grandfather David was a violin teacher, and he died before I was born. My grandmother Berta was in her thirties when she was left a penniless widow with nine children. Her sister Fani, who lived not far away in the town of Margitta (Marghita in Romanian), helped her and her children by regularly bringing them wagonloads of food.

When my mother was about eighteen or nineteen, she was shipped off to live with her Fani néni and Zismon bácsi. *Néni* and *bácsi* mean aunt and uncle in Hungarian and were the respectful names we called older people then. Zismon was an extremely religious and devout man. The idea was that living with Fani néni would afford my mother the opportunity to meet some eligible young Orthodox men and get married. Well, my mother didn't want anything to do with the young men who were brought around for her to choose from or the kind of life she would have to lead with them. She did not adhere to many of the Orthodox Jewish traditions and wouldn't marry any of the men she met. My mother was an advanced thinker, and if her family had been able to afford it, she would have continued her schooling. She had dreamed of becoming a physician. Looking back, I think that my mother was a terribly disappointed, unhappy woman.

When she came back home, her family bought a delicatessen store for her, and that's where she worked until she and my father married. My mother sold delicatessen products and fruit in that little store, which was still there when I was young. When we would pass by it, my mother would tell me that she had once owned it and worked there.

When I was a small child, maybe six or seven, my mother took me back to the town of Margitta a few times to visit her Fani néni and Zismon bácsi. Zismon bácsi had a big white beard, and he was always studying or praying. What I remember most about the house is the scent. It was a large, country-style house with a big room as the main living area. On the top of some cabinets in that room, Fani néni kept her quince preserves, which she flavoured with *etrog*, the citrus fruit used in a religious ritual during the holiday of Sukkot. Fani néni added one slice of *etrog* to each jar of quince preserves, making the house smell like a perfume factory. When I stepped into the house, the aroma of the *etrog* filled my nostrils, and I loved how it smelled.

The house had a huge back garden that sloped down to a small stream. There were fruit trees and raspberry bushes in the garden, and I would go down to the stream where there were a great many snails—tiny, tiny ones. The village children would collect the snail shells and make necklaces out of them.

My parents were married in around 1923. My mother would have been in her mid-twenties then, which was probably considered old for a girl to get married in those days. Their first child, a little girl named Eva, was born in 1924 and died at age one, three years before I was born. I don't know what she died of, but I suppose there weren't medications available at the time that could have saved her. For many years, I had a photograph of that beautiful little girl, my sister, Eva, but I don't have that photograph anymore. I tore it up many years later when my daughter, my first-born, Vicky, became ill as an infant. The photo scared me so much that I just had to do it. I regret that now, but it gave me peace then.

My mother's sister Helen died when I was around ten years old. She had epilepsy, for which there was no medication in those days. As a young woman in her twenties, she was put in a mental hospital where she lived for the rest of her life. We would visit her every Saturday morning when the weather was good enough. There was a streetcar running across town in both directions that we could have taken there, but it cost to ride it, so we walked. We had very little extra money. That was the way it was. Still, my mother always brought something special she had baked for her sister as a treat. Helena was soft-spoken, and had lovely blue eyes and a gentle demeanour. She created beautiful hand-crocheted tablecloths and other items. We would sit in the garden when we met. I was never brought inside the mental hospital.

Three of my mother's siblings, Jozsef (Jozsi), Margit and Etel, settled in Bratislava, Czechoslovakia (now Slovakia), as young adults, as jobs were more plentiful there than in Oradea. Only my mother and her sister Ilus, the youngest of the siblings, stayed in Oradea. Ilus married a kind, Christian man named Feri Kiss. Few Jewish women married Christian men in those days. Ilus had met him while working in an office as a typist when she was a young woman in the early 1920s. He was the accountant in the office. They fell in love, and even though he came from a Protestant Hungarian family, they got married. They never had children, but they had a good life together. They lived in a comfortable home and were even able to afford a helper in the house, which was a luxury. My uncle Feri was a wonderful human being. He was a tall, handsome man, straightforward, unbelievably honest and decent. He was completely accepted, loved and respected by the rest of our family.

I know even less about my father's family than I do about my mother's. My paternal grandparents lived nearby in a small village, Szentjobb (Sâniob in Romanian), and several of my father's siblings also lived in small towns or villages in the vicinity. Oddly enough, the story of my father's parents resembles that of my mother's.

My paternal grandfather, Mor Klein, had a pub in the village. One day when he was in his late thirties, he was walking home and collapsed and died of what was thought to have been a heart attack. He left his widow, who was also in her thirties, alone with seven or eight children. When her husband died, my grandmother took over the running of the pub and was able to provide for her family. She was a strong woman.

A few times when I was a child, some of my cousins and I went to stay with Granny Szentjobbi for a week in the summer. My cousins and I simply called her Granny Szentjobbi after the Hungarian name of the village. I remember her house and the pub very well. A huge berry tree graced her front yard. The berries fell everywhere, staining everything near them a deep purple, and we loved to gather and eat them.

The pub was actually a large room in the house where my grandmother lived, and it had several big round tables that could seat six to eight people each. The bar was on one side of the room with the bottles of liquor behind it, and there was often a man playing a zither to entertain the customers. In those days, the pub would have been for men only, and I remember seeing a lot of men drinking there. My grandmother would shout at anyone who got a bit loud or out of line, and no one ever crossed her.

I enjoyed visiting my grandmother. Most of the year, I was alone. When I was at her house, I saw people and all kinds of things I never saw at home. There were quite a few Jewish families who lived in Szentjobb, and I met some of them when I stayed with Granny.

3
Happy on My Own

I HAD A lonely childhood, having only my mother for company before I started school, but I don't remember feeling loneliness as a child. I didn't know that there was any other kind of life. I was timid and shy, and awkward in company. I had no social skills and even had difficulty playing with my cousins. If they got too loud or too wild, it scared me. They once locked the door to their apartment and told me I couldn't go home. All I wanted was to get away from them, from people who wanted to do something I didn't want to do.

I was usually happy being alone. That was my life, and I was not in my cousins' or friends' homes often enough to see the differences between their lives and mine. The rare time I saw a mother being playful and funny was at my friend Nelly's house. Nelly's mother wasn't often at home because she had taken over her husband's travelling sales job when he went blind, and she became the breadwinner. The few times she was at home, she was always smiling and joking. I couldn't get over what a happy, light personality she had. I was amazed and in awe that a mother could be like that. My mother was with me all the time, but we didn't really interact. She was involved with her cooking or chores, and she read novels in the evenings. So that was what I did too. When I was supposed to be studying, I read my library books.

I didn't know what to do with dolls and didn't like playing with them, but I learned to love books and the couple of old board games that we had. I taught myself to read in Hungarian before I started school. Books became my world and how I discovered the world. I didn't learn as much in school or from my mother. I especially loved Hungarian authors, not necessarily the famous ones they taught us in school. My favourite books were historical novels about life in royal courts and aristocratic homes—stories of troubled maidens who were supposed to get married to someone they didn't love though they were in love with the servant in the house or someone like that. My mind was opened to different countries and different lives and times. I also liked Greek mythology and poetry.

When I was quite young, I was given a little case of watercolours by an older cousin, Rozsika, who came to live with us for a year. I liked to paint, but I was so careful about it because I knew that if I used up the paints, I would not be able to replace them. I learned to draw very delicate, small things, like flowers, leaves and decorations, and that gave me joy. I still paint sometimes.

As a child, it was difficult for me to speak up for myself, and I rarely asked for anything. The only time I remember getting what I wanted was when I was ten, and my parents decided that I should learn an instrument. They chose the violin, but I said, "No, I don't like the violin. I love the piano."

There was not much music in my life in the early years, but when I was about six or seven, we got a radio, and I was able to listen to the philharmonic orchestra playing concerts from Budapest with different pianists and violinists. I liked that very much, especially the piano solos. So, when it came to learning music, I didn't want to hear about the screechy violin; I wanted to learn to play the piano. We couldn't afford to buy a piano when I started, so I practised at my teacher's house after school for the first year.

Then my aunt Helen died. I received some of her money, and my parents got me my own piano. I was allowed to choose which one I wanted. There were many beautiful upright pianos at the shop that were suitable for our small apartment, but when I saw the Stingl baby grand and played a few scales on it, I wanted it. It had a beautiful sound and was about the same price as the uprights, so my parents said I could have it. Once I finally got my own piano, my parents didn't have to tell me to practice. I loved playing and practised for two or three hours every day. Until about twenty years ago, I would occasionally sit down and play Chopin or Beethoven's Moonlight Sonata or some of my other favourites.

4
Friendship

ORADEA WAS A beautiful city that had the Körös River (Criş River in Romanian) running right through the middle of it, dividing it almost in half. It had large, elaborate churches. One of them was called the Moon Church because a mechanism installed in the church tower turned to show the phases of the moon. In the middle of town, there was a beautiful open square, Szent László Tér (St. Ladislaus Square), named after King Ladislaus, who founded the city in the eleventh century, and there was a children's playground in it.

Hungary and Romania both claimed Oradea as theirs, and when Hungary was on the losing side of World War I, it was given to Romania. But, in my grandparents' and my parents' time, the population of the city was mostly Hungarian speaking.

There were about twenty thousand Jews in the city of ninety-three thousand people, but unlike the Jews of Poland and the rest of Eastern Europe, we didn't speak Yiddish at home. We spoke Hungarian, and so did everyone else in my world. When it came to culture, the language of the time was German. Some of the Hungarians, the aristocrats and wealthy landholders, didn't even speak Hungarian. They spoke German and had *Fräuleins*, young women who worked as nannies to take care of the children and teach them German.

When I was about five, I was sent to a German kindergarten where they spoke Hungarian to the children and taught German. I don't remember learning a word of German there, but I do remember watching a puppet show of "Little Red Riding Hood" at that kindergarten. I was very afraid of the Big Bad Wolf, which looked like a dog to me. I had no pets at all in my life, and I was always afraid of dogs. When I went out on the street with my mother and dogs barked at me, I was terrified.

By the time I turned six, I was in Grade 1 at the Orthodox Jewish all-girls' school. Most of the other kids were one year older, but my mother got a special dispensation from our family doctor for me to start school early. My school was separated into two buildings on different streets, one for girls and one for boys. The boys' school was about a block away from the main synagogue. The girls' school was the same school my mother had attended and where she had learned German. In her time, there were only eight grades. By my time, the school had added on grades, so you could go from there straight to university.

Our classes were taught in Romanian. I remember my mother helping me to learn how to pronounce some of the letters and words that were different than Hungarian. French, German and Latin were added to the curriculum in Grade 5. I enjoyed learning, especially history, geography, literature and art, which I loved. I was fine with basic math too, but more complicated maths like algebra and geometry were beyond me. When I tried to learn them, my brain didn't take the information in. Nothing penetrated, and I felt stupid and insecure.

When I started school, I was exposed to other children's company. I was inexperienced at making new friends, and it took me a long time to be able to interact with groups, though I liked the companionship of my classmates. School was a comfortable atmosphere for me because I was surrounded by the same girls who went from grade to grade together. I wonder how I came to a place where I can now talk about my life and intimate things with groups of people. I am so different now from what I used to feel and be like. Now, my story just pours out of me. It took until almost my eightieth year for that to happen.

When I was six, we lived at Liliom Utca 6, in a small, one-storey private house that was divided into two apartments in the front, with another small apartment built in the back of the inner courtyard. In the front were the landlord's and our apartments. The windows faced the street, but the entrances were through the back garden along a small walkway covered in morning glory. At the back of the garden was the third little apartment. Our apartment had two large rooms. The kitchen and living room were at the front, and the bedroom was at the back. The three of us slept there — my parents in a bed and me, initially, in a crib and then on a small sofa bed.

I made one friend in Grade 1 — Iboya, whose family's small apartment was at the back of the garden we lived off of. We were not a well-to-do household by any means, but I was shocked when Iboya first took me to her apartment after school. Their front room was a kitchen, like in our apartment, but our kitchen had big windows with lots of light, and hers had only a small window with very little light. There was just a bare table with a couple of chairs, and it looked so dark and depressing. Neither of her parents were at home, which surprised me. She was six and nobody was there to take care of her when she got home from school.

Iboya was hungry so she started a fire in the wood stove and took out a couple of potatoes. That was all there was in the house, not even bread. She sliced the potatoes up into thin little slices and cooked them on top of the stove. Then her little sister, who was about four, came out of the bedroom, and all three of us had these little pieces of potato to eat.

I was in awe that Iboya's parents allowed her to start a fire and cut potatoes with a big knife. I found out later that her parents were peddlers and went around with a wagon from one place to another to sell goods. They were often gone for days, and Iboya looked after her little sister all by herself. She was able to do things for herself and make food for herself. I wasn't allowed to even go near fire, so I admired her greatly.

When I was about seven or eight, we moved to Várady Zsigmond Utca 8. I didn't mingle with the neighbours, whether they were Jewish or not. For me it was either school or home, studying or reading—mostly reading novels from the public library while pretending to study. All in all, I accepted whatever came along. I didn't see my friend from the old house anymore. I lived totally in the moment, and so it didn't really matter to me. I continued going to the same school and walked there even though it was farther than it was from our old apartment.

Our new place was an apartment in a building that surrounded a courtyard. The street-facing part of the building had two or three storeys and a wide entrance into the large, open courtyard. On the other three sides of the courtyard were one-storey apartments, and our new apartment was one of these. We had two rooms, as well as a tiny kitchen and a bathroom. Each tenant had a small space in the courtyard where they could cultivate their own flowers. The rest of the courtyard was dedicated to a children's playground where all the children played. That's where I learned to play chess and Rummikub. Everyone played chess and Rummikub then.

We always lived on the same side of the Körös River. Our whole family lived in the same neighbourhood. My school was on the same side of the river and the market, as well as the pharmacy, our family doctor and my father's woodworking shop.

In Grade 2, I made a new friend, Hajnal Schwartz. She was an only child like me, and we usually went to her place after school even though her mother was never at home. We preferred to go there because she had a private backyard with a swing. Her mother made great big jars of apricot jam which we ate spoonfuls of. What a treat that was.

Then we moved again when I was around ten, this time, to an apartment on the second floor of a building at Teleki Pál Utca 44. I became best friends with a girl who shared my name, Hedy, and lived next door. We were also classmates. There were three apartments on every floor and a basement where the janitor lived. The building had a backyard where there were sheds in which firewood was kept for the winter.

Our new apartment was what my mother had always wanted. It was more spacious and had big windows that looked out on the street, a balcony and a much bigger bathroom with a separate little room for the toilet and a large hallway entrance. The smaller room was my parents' bedroom. I slept in the living room on a sofa that my father had made which opened up into a bed. The hallway was quite large, big enough to have a small dining table in it, and we usually ate there or at the kitchen table.

The main room was large enough to accommodate my piano, the dining room table—where we had our special holiday dinners and where I occasionally played card games with my parents—and a large wall unit my father had made. It also had a *cserépkályha*, a large clay stove going from the floor almost to the ceiling. The stove was covered in beige ceramic tiles and had bricks for insulation on the inside. This kind of stove was used for heating, and it was the only way to keep warm in the winter. Auntie Ilus had a unit like ours, but hers was covered in beautiful carved green tiles that fascinated me.

My auntie Ilus had no children, and she was often alone because of her husband's work. Even though he was originally an accountant in the factory where they met, by this time he was a travelling salesman and went around Transylvania to all the small towns, selling a unique Hungarian product called Diana Sósborszesz. It was an alcoholic liquid that was used as a digestive elixir. Even a little drop on a cube of sugar was supposed to cure whatever ailed you. It also came in the form of chocolate bonbons, which were filled with a little bit of this liquid. This was a fantastic job for Uncle Feri because Diana was *the* product of the time, and he made a good living selling it. The only drawback was that he was away from home a lot.

5
The Accident

IN THE SUMMER of 1939, when I was eleven, my father had a terrible accident. We were at a pool and he dove into the shallow end instead of the deep end and hit his head. I was in the pool with him at the time, and when I noticed his head bobbing in the water, I thought he was joking around, as he did sometimes. But when I picked up his head and let it go again, it fell back, and I realized something was terribly wrong. I started crying out and calling for help. I stayed with him until the grown-ups took over and pulled him out. They held him upside down to drain water out of him, and then they gave him artificial resuscitation until the ambulance came and took him to the hospital.

After the accident, I was sent away for a month to stay with my father's brother Sandor, his wife, Olga, and their two children, Marika and Laicsi. They had a nice summer house near Váradszentmárton (Sânmartin in Romanian), in the little community around Félixfürdő (Băile Felix), where there were healing thermal springs and spas where people came to receive treatments. Many people, those who could afford it, would spend a week or two there every summer. It was supposed to rejuvenate you and keep you healthy because the water was full of beneficial minerals. When I was there, we all slept in one big room in the back of the house, where there was a large bed for my uncle and aunt, a small bed for Marika and another small bed for Laicsi. They put another small bed in the room for me.

The house was surrounded by trees and had quite a large grassy area around it. It was a ten-minute walk to the spa, where there was an open thermal pool in which a machine made mechanical waves every half hour. There were nice walkways there too, as well as a photography shop, coffee houses and restaurants, all surrounded by forests.

I stayed with my aunt and uncle until things got sorted out with my father. They were nice to me, and the children included me in their games even though we weren't very close before that and I had only met them every four to six weeks for an hour or two when the family got together. They did go to the same school as I did, but Laicsi was in the boy's school and Marika was two or three years younger than me and in a lower grade. During that summer, we played all sorts of games together and walked on the forest trails. I loved the green open spaces and nature. I had come from the city, from an apartment on a paved street with a neglected backyard that had no real garden, few plants and trees. The forest was heaven for me.

6
Warnings

IN SEPTEMBER 1939, the war began, but it did not affect us directly initially. A year later, Northern Transylvania, including Oradea, was handed over to Hungary. Oradea was again called by its Hungarian name, Nagyvárad, and the language of our school instantly changed from Romanian to Hungarian.

My father eventually went back to work but his accident had caused damage to the vertebrae at the top of his spine, and that reduced his ability to lift his arms. His gait changed too, and he had to walk with a cane for balance. He was not able to work as much as he had, but, strangely, things got a little better for us financially. Either he figured out how to make more income from his work or there was less competition at that point because many Jewish men were being taken away to the forced labour service. My father was exempt because of his injury. I lived a quiet, sheltered life with little exposure to media, and I had no inkling of what was going on in the world around me.

Then, in 1942, my mother's older sister Margit, who lived in Bratislava, came to visit. I found out after the war that Margit had come to warn us. Slovakia was collaborating with Germany to deport its Jews, and everything had changed. Jews were being grabbed off the street and taken away to concentration camps to await transport to Auschwitz and other Nazi camps. It became dangerous to go outside, but people had no choice since they had to buy food and other essentials. When her husband and the children were taken away, Margit began selling furniture and other items from the apartment to have money to bribe the guards and release her family. But they kept getting arrested, until finally she ran out of things to sell and wasn't able to get them out any longer. Margit's husband, her two girls and young boy were eventually all taken away.

Margit decided she was not going to stay in Bratislava to await the same fate as her family. She wanted to go to Oradea to be with her sisters and warn them about what was happening in the rest of Europe. But she didn't have false papers to leave the country or a passport and visa to travel. So, she dressed up as a peasant woman, all in black with a large cross on her chest and a black scarf on her head, and tried to make herself look as old as possible. Then she went to the train station and bought a ticket, heading to Oradea. On the journey, she sat in the corner, hunched over, and pretended to be asleep. When the authorities came in to ask everyone for their papers, the other people in the compartment felt sorry for her and told them to leave the old woman alone. No one questioned her further or stopped her. She was fortunate.

I was not aware of this at the time, but Margit arrived in Oradea and told the family what had happened in Bratislava, which was not that far away, warning them that it would happen to us too. Hitler was going to come to Hungary. She urged us to prepare, to get out and go to Switzerland or Romania if we could. But my parents did not believe Jews would be targeted in the same way in Hungary. Nobody did, it seemed. We were Hungarian, and being Jewish wasn't even a priority for my family. We weren't that religious and we didn't live a particularly Jewish life. We got along well with everyone. There were villages in the northeast of the country where very Orthodox Jews lived like they did in the shtetls of Poland and Lithuania. But it was like those places were in a different country. We were Hungarian city people, very different from the religious communities in the northeast.

We lit Shabbat candles and went to synagogue maybe three times a year: on Rosh Hashanah, Yom Kippur and maybe once more. And that was it as far as our Jewishness went. That's how most of us lived in our family circle. My mother had a kosher kitchen but my father had no problem occasionally sidestepping it because Auntie Ilus often had nice kielbasa and sausages at her house around Christmas, and he loved that. He was proud that he had been a Hungarian soldier who fought for Hungary in World War I. "I was a soldier," my father said. "I was injured and bled for my country. They would not betray me; they would not betray us."

Margit warned them to be prepared, but they simply could not imagine that the same thing could happen to them. Not in Hungary. It was possible for some people who had money and connections to leave. I found out later that a classmate of mine and her whole family all survived because they went to Romania the day before the Nazis came to take us to the ghetto. But that possibility was not for ordinary people like us. We didn't have money to get to another country or relatives there to give us a home. And, even if we did, my father, with his disability, would not have been able to make that illegal and dangerous journey. How would we have been able to get smuggled across the border? You had to be agile and well. None of it was possible for our family.

At that time, I had no idea about anything that was happening in the world. I was sent out of the room when the adults were talking. Though I was aware that something was going on, it seemed far away and irrelevant to my life, to my parents' lives or to our community. I was oblivious. Many adults didn't tell children anything in those days. Children should not know bad things, should not worry, the thinking went. No one talked to me about what was going on. I never did hear, at home or at school, about the war or about antisemitic incidents in the world. In fact, I didn't even hear the word "antisemitism" until 1944, when it was associated with Hitler. I knew nothing that would have made me realize there was danger or that would have shattered my idea of having an ideal life of parents, home and school in a safe community.

Margit stayed with us a week or two. There was nothing to go back home to, so she decided she would stay close to her sisters and go to work. She had always supported herself before, so she was prepared to do it again. She put an ad in the paper for work as a nanny and was hired by a wealthy Jewish family in a small village somewhere near Oradea.

She stayed with this family for about two years, until 1944, when the Jews in the area were taken into a former brick factory that was turned into a ghetto. But Margit managed to escape. Milk was delivered to the brickyard every morning in large metal canisters like the ones peasant women carried on their backs. The canisters were emptied of milk, washed and then left to be picked up the next day, when fresh milk was delivered. Margit took out her black dress and coat, her big cross and her black babushka kerchief. She put one of those empty containers on her back and simply walked to the train station. Again, she had no papers, but she didn't look stereotypically Jewish. Margit got a ticket and took the train back to Oradea. She arrived at the end of May, missing my mother, my father and me by only one day.

Margit stayed with Ilus for few days and then told her she didn't want to endanger her. She put on her black clothes and cross again, took the empty canister on her back and got a train to Bratislava. She somehow found a way to hide for a few days before getting a job as a nanny for the family of a German Nazi officer. She told them she was a Christian and had lost her papers in the bombings. That's how she survived the war.

Margit was the only one who told us the truth about what was happening. Even our leaders, religious and secular, didn't warn us. They couldn't bring themselves to believe. When people asked for advice, the Jewish leaders said, "Just do what the law says, what the government says. Everything will be all right. Don't rock the boat." Only the young people in the Zionist youth groups were aware of the danger that lay ahead. I later found out from my husband, who had been a member of one of those groups, that they believed the rumours about the horrors that Jews would be facing in Hungary and were ready to go to Palestine. But their parents wouldn't listen to them. The older generations believed they were equal citizens of their country. They said, "Don't listen to the Zionists. Everything's going to be all right. Don't worry."

When I was fifteen, a classmate of mine invited me over to her house for a get-together with a few girls and boys one weekend. I wouldn't even have dared to ask my mother if I could invite boys to my house. That day, I met Leslie (Laci) Dan, who was four years older than me. He had already finished high school and wanted to become a physician. He was handsome, kind and intelligent. Laci walked me home and asked if I would go for a walk with him the next weekend. I said yes, and we met again and started going for walks in the park and along the river that ran through the city. Sometimes we would go down to the river and walk near the shore. He would hold my hand, and it was sweet and romantic but we didn't even kiss. Our relationship was very short-lived though because a few months later we were all forced into an overcrowded ghetto with the rest of the Jews of Oradea.

7
The Ghetto

WITHIN TWO OR three weeks of the Nazis occupying Hungary in 1944, they took over the government and replaced the liberal mayor of our city with a Nazi, just like they did everywhere else in Hungary. It was then that one of the special units of Hungarian soldiers, the *csendőrség* (gendarmerie, or police force), who wore hats with a rooster feather on it, became the real representatives of Nazism.

My school was closed in March without warning. One day, we were all called into the auditorium. The principal stood before us and announced that the school would close, effective immediately, and that he hoped we would see each other again after the war. No explanation was given. We were simply told to go home. The closing of Jewish schools was the latest in a string of anti-Jewish laws that restricted our rights and freedoms, one law at a time. Radios were one of the first things to be confiscated. We were no longer allowed to listen to the news. There was a law that forbade Jewish students from attending college or university. I knew this because there were a couple of young Jewish men now working for my father, apprenticed to him because they couldn't go to university or enter better professions or businesses.

I missed going to school, but we still could walk out on the streets. I wasn't aware in the slightest of what was going on until, in April 1944, my mother sewed a yellow Star of David on my coat. That's when I felt marked for the first time. Still, I had no inkling of what was to come. I couldn't understand why we were being singled out. I wondered what we had done—my parents and the other Jews—to warrant it. Even then, my parents didn't explain anything to me, and I was confused as to why I couldn't go to school and why we had to wear the star. I don't remember if I asked questions. If I did, there were no answers provided. I suppose my parents were trying to protect me from fear and the brutal reality of what the rumours suggested. Everything was changing so quickly, it was bewildering.

Every week, new anti-Jewish laws came out, laws that took everything away from us: our homes, our possessions, our freedom and our rights to citizenship and humane treatment. We had to go to city hall and hand over the contents of our bank accounts. Jews were no longer entitled to have anything of value, and the Nazis demanded that all valuables be handed in—paintings, sculptures, furs and jewellery. They started arresting Jews and torturing them in the police stations if they thought they were hiding money or valuable possessions. If a Jew was known to be wealthy and the Nazis thought they hadn't given up enough, they were tortured.

Jewish businesses were taken over by the Nazis, but my father's workshop wasn't confiscated. I suppose the small workshop wasn't important enough or productive or rich enough to be of any note. They left it alone, and my father had it until we went into the ghetto, just several weeks after we started wearing the yellow star.

I barely remember those last weeks at home before we were forced into the ghetto. I was probably reading and playing piano. I don't even remember visiting with my classmates. I do remember seeing Laci though. He came to see me even though most people were afraid to walk on the streets by then. Wearing the yellow star meant you would be recognized as a Jew and get beaten up, or worse. The star became an open invitation for anyone who wanted to abuse Jews without repercussions, rather with the encouragement of all those around.

When we knew we were going to be moving to a ghetto, I put together my memory book, my most treasured possession. It was a simple, small book with blank drawing pages that my mother and father had given me on my eleventh birthday. They had inscribed in it a message of love and encouragement for me. I asked my close friends to draw a special picture in my memory book for me and several did. That book survived the war, and I look at those pictures now and wonder about the lives my friends could have lived.

We took my memory book and a few other precious possessions, including our family photographs and my mother's brooch and necklace, to Ilus and Feri's apartment. We also brought over my Stingl baby grand piano, my treasure. They only had two rooms and a kitchen and bathroom in their apartment, so they shoehorned the piano into a corner of their bedroom because the living room already had a dining table and chairs, a large sofa and two armchairs and a table where they played their chess games every night. Ilus also had the footstool that my father had made for her. Otherwise, during those weeks, I was mostly at home, except if my mother sent me out to the grocery store or the baker, which were both close to where we lived.

By early May, we were forced to quickly leave our homes and move into the newly created Jewish ghetto, leaving almost everything behind. Around twenty-seven thousand of the city's thirty thousand Jews were confined to a number of city blocks around which a tall solid wood perimeter fence was constructed. The Jews were forced into that space, carrying only what they could. My father wasn't able to carry very much, but we weren't allowed to take much anyway, only a little suitcase each. I was told to pack a bag and take a dress, pyjamas, a coat, soap and a toothbrush. Minimal things. My mother packed blankets and a change of clothes. One of the gendarmes came up to our apartment and forced us out. I remember the janitor came up to our apartment with him, and as we were going out, she rolled up our hall carpet and took it away with her. The gendarme had our apartment key, and when we left, he locked the door and pocketed the key. He marched us down the steps and to an open truck that was waiting in front of the building. We were told to climb up into it. It took about ten minutes to drive to the ghetto.

We were taken to an apartment in a three-storey building. I believe it was in the same building we had previously lived in on Várady Zsigmond Utca. The apartment had two or three bedrooms, and we were led into one of the bedrooms. It was not a big room, but I remember thinking that it wasn't so bad. Then we were told, "That corner is yours." In the other three corners were three other families. We put our few belongings down in our corner and slept crowded on the floor. There was a kitchen in the apartment, and we must have had some food, but there were about twelve families living there in one apartment, and there wasn't much to go around.

Strangely, the transition to the ghetto wasn't as traumatic for me as one might think. We were in a prison, crowded and bewildered, but I had my parents with me so I was not afraid. I believed I would be safe as long as my parents were with me. I never imagined a life that wasn't a continuation of what I knew—one with my parents, my auntie, my classmates.

Even though we were now in the ghetto, we were still in denial. We were told that the government was going to take us to the border and we were going to work there for farmers or factories until the end of the war, and then we would be able to come back home. That was the story. That anyone could believe it is still a wonder. But we chose to believe it because the alternative was unthinkable.

We were in the ghetto for about four weeks, until the end of May. I turned sixteen on May 11, but I didn't celebrate. I can't tell you what I did there all day before we were all taken away. We were allowed to leave our apartments and walk within the fenced-in area of the ghetto, which I did a couple of times when Laci came over and we went out together. We also met one of my classmates, Erzsok, the one who had introduced me to Laci. All I really remember of that time is that corner of the bedroom where my parents and I slept on the floor and seeing Laci and Erzsok.

The deportations started about two weeks after our arrival in the ghetto, and house after house, apartment building after apartment building was emptied out daily. Within three or four weeks, the whole ghetto, thousands every day, had been shipped out. The Hungarian collaborators were so vicious, they are said to have surpassed even the Germans in their cruelty. I don't remember seeing more than half a dozen German soldiers in the city, but there were thousands of Hungarians who did everything in their power to humiliate us and take away from us our homes and businesses, our dignity and our lives. The hatred I felt, the resentment and anger toward the Hungarians was only bearable because of my wonderful uncle, who was also a Hungarian. I reminded myself of that.

When they came for us, they told us we had to leave our suitcases; we couldn't even take them with us. I think my mother had a large bag that she took with her, but I don't know what she carried in it. My father and I had nothing. We were marched to the trains and jammed into the cattle cars, so many people that there was no room for anything else. I was with my mother and father, so I didn't worry about where we were going. Wherever they went, as long as I could go with them, I would be okay. How naive and foolish I was.

I had never heard a word about what was going on in Poland, about what was happening in the Polish ghettos. Nothing. Later, I was told that the Hungarian Zionist organizations had been sending money to the synagogues in Poland to buy food for the Polish Jews in the ghettos and that the last shipment had come back. The courier told them that everything and everyone was gone; there was no one left.

Some people had to have known what was happening but kept it to themselves. It wasn't made public. I think they were afraid that we would panic and revolt and cause problems. The leaders of the synagogues and social and professional communities must have thought that the Nazis would shoot us all if we caused problems. And everyone else who must have known, including my parents, still didn't want to believe it. Until the last moment, my father felt he was more Hungarian than Jewish, and he was proud to be Hungarian. He thought the Hungarians would never betray us.

It took only three months from the time the schools closed until we were taken away. What happened during that short time in Hungary had taken two years in other parts of Europe. By the time we were taken, all of the work-aged men had already been taken away to work in forced labour battalions, so the cattle cars were filled mostly with women with babies and children, old people, people with disabilities and sick people. We were shoved into the cattle cars and were in there for three days and three nights—standing room only, shoulder to shoulder, packed in, close to a hundred of us. I had someone right up against me, in front of me, behind me and on both sides of me. But that journey of three days and nights in the cattle car was much more difficult for my mother than it was for me. I remember that she couldn't breathe well and I fanned her with a handkerchief. It wasn't until after the first or second day that she was finally able to wiggle into a squat against the wall of the car.

We had been given a single pail of water and an empty pail for the toilet, but there was no empty corner to put it in and nothing to cover it with. The water was gone within an hour. At some point, I had to squat down over that pail. Very soon it overflowed. There were some spaces between the slats on the floor, and people tried to pour its contents out, but that wasn't successful. The stench was terrible. The babies were crying, and the old people were sick and moaning all around us, already worn out by life and what they had been through, what they were being put through now. The darkness was horrible. There was just a little bit of light and air coming through the little window high up on one side of the cattle car.

I don't remember, in all those three days and nights, one word spoken between me and my mother and father. If there was, I wish I could remember what was said. But I don't. It is a blank.

8
Left Standing

WHEN WE ARRIVED at Auschwitz-Birkenau at the beginning of June 1944, I was shocked by what I saw and heard, confused, bewildered. I looked around on that sunny day and didn't know what I was looking at, never mind where I was. I didn't know what this huge place, with its large barracks were for. What purpose did they serve? Why were we there?

Everyone poured out of the trains, hungry and thirsty, haggard, desperate and exhausted. We had been standing and squatting in misery in those cattle cars for three days and nights without food or water. At best, we looked awful but surely much worse than that. And then there were those Nazi soldiers, so spiffy and clean, hair slicked down, uniforms pressed and boots shiny. From the first moment, we were treated as subhuman by all of them. We were screamed at, yelled at, cursed at: "Verfluchte Juden!"—*Cursed Jews!* "Schweinejuden"—*Jew pigs!* they called us. There was no talking to us, just screaming insults and orders.

As soon as we were out of the trains, everything moved so quickly, like a nightmare in fast-forward. Seconds after we got out of the cattle cars, there were shouts for the men to go to the left. My father was suddenly gone and was standing with the men and boys. We never even said goodbye. I never saw him again.

My mind was reeling as I stood there looking around at all those barracks, dozens of them on the left and the right—separated by electrified wire fences on all sides. I had never seen or heard anything that would have prepared me to understand where I was. Perhaps a minute went by while my mind tried to process what I was doing there. In that minute, while I was not paying attention, orders were given for the women to move, and I suddenly realized that my mother had moved ahead. She was walking about ten rows ahead of me with a group of older women and young mothers holding babies or holding the hands of their young children. I couldn't understand it. Where were they going, and why was my mother going without me? I started running to catch up and join her when a young Nazi soldier stopped me in mid-stride, held a rifle in front of me and said: "Nein!"—*No!*

I just looked at him. He pointed and told me to go to the right with some young women. I looked toward my mother, and then I looked at him and I said in German, "No, no. I have to go with my mother. She's there." I pointed to her.

He said, "Nein!" again, and his rifle didn't move.

That's when I shouted after my mother. I was being ripped apart inside. She heard my scream and turned around, and we looked at each other. I don't know what I expected, maybe that she would come and get me and tell the Nazi soldier not to stop me, to let me go and join her. Whatever I expected was not what happened. We just looked at each other, my mother and me, and then, without a word, she turned and kept walking away, and I was left standing there. I was stunned.

Maybe my mother knew that if I came to her, I would have to go to the gas chamber. Maybe that's why she didn't speak to me or ask me to come to her. I honestly don't know. I cannot imagine what she must have gone through to see her only child in such circumstances—and her husband, disabled, with no hope of surviving the work routine that might be waiting for him. She was forty-eight years old and my father was fifty, which seemed old to me then.

Did my mother know where she was walking to? Did she think then about the warning that her sister Margit had given her? Or was she just dazed, worn out by the degradation she had just suffered—three days in the dark, dehydrated? Was she at the end of her strength, and did she just give up?

I've asked myself these questions many times. But I'll never know.

I didn't know what hit me as we were taken into the first barracks on the right, which was a disinfection area. I was, for the first time, without my mother's protection and guidance. We were told to take all our clothes off. Our clothes were taken away, and we were sent to the showers, about fifty or sixty of us at a time. I imagine it was the same for my parents and all the others who were taken into the gas chambers, into the same type of room with grey concrete walls, a concrete floor and no windows, shower heads on the concrete ceiling. Our shower heads, when they were turned on, produced water.

We were not given towels when we came out of the showers, scared, naked and wet. We were ordered to go into the next room, which was a very large room. There were men waiting there, and they were watching us come in. A few short months earlier, I had been an innocent teenage girl, a high school student. Now, I was here in some unknown hell, which I later learned was Auschwitz-Birkenau, naked and wet, without parents, paraded in front of a group of men. I was lost and horrified.

The men then shaved our heads and then all our body hair, including our pubic hair. Then they blew some kind of disinfectant powder at our genitals, front and back. They told us to go to a long table that was piled high with what looked like rags but were actually clothes that must have been taken from the arrivals before us, just as our clothes were probably given to the transport to come in after us. As we walked by, someone threw a garment at each of us. Just like that: pick one up, throw; pick one up, throw. If it fit, you were lucky. Some people were heavy and got a dress for a skinny woman. Some were tiny and got a huge dress. I got a little cotton dress with a Scotch plaid pattern in blue and burgundy, and nothing to wear under it. No panties, no slip, no bra, no socks. There were piles of old shoes to quickly choose from. I got a pair of wooden-soled clogs that fit okay, and I was glad to have them.

9
My Reflection

WHEN WE EMERGED, we were told to go and find a place in any of the barracks where there was room. We didn't get tattooed as I later learned others had been. I don't know if they didn't have the time or they just figured there was no point in numbering and keeping track of us anymore. Why bother? We would all die soon.

About half a dozen young women around my age were walking together. We didn't speak, but we all just walked out of there together and started looking for a barracks to park ourselves in as we had been ordered to do. We were in a grey place with no colour. Everything was drab beyond words. There was not one flower or bush, not one tree, not a blade of grass or leaf. As we were walking in the middle of this enormous camp, we passed a barracks on the left, number 15, which had one window at eye level. The sun was out and shining on the window. It was like a mirror, and as we came upon it, we all stopped and looked in the window. When I looked, I didn't see myself. I saw strange, bald, skinny women. I didn't know which one in the group was me. I couldn't tell until I counted. One, two, three, four people in the window. One, two, three, four — looking at us. That fourth bald girl was me? I couldn't believe it. Three days earlier, I had been removed from under an umbrella of love and care that I'd felt my entire life from my parents. Now I was someone else, someone unrecognizable to me.

Then we disbursed as one girl found a place here and another one found a place there. I found myself in one of the last barracks in the area where we were being held. This barracks had no windows, just huge doors, like barn doors, and wooden walls. There were no floors, just earth, the same as outside. Our good fortune was that it was summer and we weren't in Auschwitz-Birkenau in the winter without any extra clothing or blankets, especially when we stood outdoors for *Appell*, roll call, for several hours, as we were forced to do twice daily.

There were women lying on the floor side by side in the barracks, and I saw an empty spot. Prisoners were coming into Birkenau so fast that, in some of the barracks, they hadn't built the tiered bed structures that were in other barracks, and people just lay on the ground. No one complained; the women just lay there. I went to the space I had spotted and lay down. A few days later, it rained, and I realized why that space had not been taken. The roof above it was leaking, and the earth I was lying on became a puddle—a muddy, cold puddle. The voice in my head said, *No, you can't lie down there. It's suicide. You'll get sick.* So, after roll call, I wandered out and walked around the barracks. I found three little pieces of scrap wood left over from the construction of the barracks, I assume. I had my solution. When I lay down, I put one little piece of wood under my knees, one under my hips and one under my shoulders, and I was raised up about half an inch above the puddle, just high enough to keep somewhat dry.

There was no chance of escape, no thoughts about it. Since we weren't taken out of the camp to work, there was no place to go. There was a tower in the middle of the camp where a Nazi guard with a machine gun stood watch, and we were warned not to go near the electrified wire fences. If we did, we would be shot. But I did go near it. Someone must have told me that in the next camp there were people from Czechoslovakia, and I thought maybe my cousins from Bratislava would be there. So, I went to the fence sometimes and shouted their names. But no one answered, and I never found anyone.

Totally alone.

10
Focusing on Survival

I ATE WHATEVER and however much I was given. It was not enough to survive on. For meals, we received a so-called soup that was our only daily food except for a little piece of bread. There was nothing in the soup that could be thought of as nourishing, or even as food—no meat, no potatoes, no vegetables. It was a brown liquid with little wooden twigs in it, and it tasted like it looked—awful. When I swallowed the soup, it left a sandy residue on my tongue. On my first day, when I stood in line waiting for my turn to receive a bowl of soup, I saw the girl in front of me not drinking it when they gave it to her. She took a sip and burst into tears. But I immediately thought that my mother would want me to drink it in case there was some nourishment in it, and so I was determined to force myself. As I drank it, I cried and held my nose, but I swallowed the whole thing.

I concentrated on trying to stay clean and healthy. Early every morning, I went to the huge, empty washroom, took off my dress and shoes, and washed with ice-cold water from head to toe. I knew it was important to be clean, so I did that religiously without missing a day. I was surprised that I was mostly alone when I was washing. No one else found within themselves whatever it was that got me up early morning before roll call to wash with cold water.

And I drank that horrible soup every day. They also gave us some kind of coffee substitute, and I drank some of that too. At home, I'd have poured it down the sink. About two or three weeks after I got to Auschwitz, I noticed having loose bowel movements. I knew that if you got diarrhea it could mean dysentery, and then you would be taken out of the camp never to return, as was happening with others. I remembered that when I was a child my mother would give me a bit of charcoal to eat if I had diarrhea, so I went wandering around outside the barracks looking for a burnt piece of wood. I eventually found a piece of charred wood. I chewed on the charred part of the wood, and I got better.

I was doing all of this so that I could be with my mother again when it was all over. I was sure that she was okay and was doing the same things I was doing to survive. If I had realized what had happened to her, I wouldn't have been able to go on. My innocence and naïveté had no bounds, and I couldn't look the danger and horror of that place in the face. I lived in hell and I didn't know it, didn't see the terrible cruelty that other survivors of Auschwitz-Birkenau witnessed and talk about. Being alone, I only concentrated on my own needs. Everything else was secondary to my desire to stay healthy and survive so I could be reunited with my mother when it was over. Not *if* it was over, *when* it was over. My situation awakened in me an ability I had never needed before—the ability to improvise, to go on, to survive.

I didn't think of my attitude as courageous for one moment, and it surprises me when I hear people refer to it that way. It was instinct, an immediate reaction to my need for my family, for my mother. I had to believe that it wasn't over, and I had to continue, no matter what. I created this belief in my mind that my mother was in a camp just like I was. Remembering the forced labour battalions that the young men had been taken to at the beginning of the war, I thought that would be our fate too, my parents' and mine—even though I knew in my heart that my father would not make it, not with his disability. But I knew my mother would be able to do it. She was strong and intelligent and would stay alive. So, I told myself that I would be reunited with my mother at least. And I believed that the only thing that would prevent me from being with my mother at the end of the war was if I didn't survive it.

By the time I came to Auschwitz-Birkenau, none of the inmates in our area of the camp worked, unless you count the roll calls work—the two or three hours, twice a day, standing without moving or talking, with armed guards enforcing the rules, just so that we could be counted. We were in a holding tank. We did nothing day in and day out, just wandered around, trying to survive on the minimal food they gave us.

One of the first people I saw in the camp when I was walking around was Erzsok, the girl who had introduced me to Laci. While the rest of us were bald, she had a pink triangular kerchief on her head. I understood that she had some kind of elevated position in her barracks and had a connection with the *Blockälteste*, the prisoner appointed by the Nazi authorities as the supervisor of a barracks. These women had relatively privileged positions. They were responsible for the behaviour of the other prisoners and had the authority to punish them. Erzsok didn't even said hello to me when I saw her.

I met two of my other childhood friends in Birkenau. When I saw Hedy Neumann, my best friend, she looked very unwell. I told her that we had to stay healthy and how I made myself swallow that horrible liquid they gave us that they called soup. No matter how horrible it was, we had to drink it. But she said, "I am hungry and thirsty, but I cannot swallow it. I just can't."

I only saw my best friend that once, and then she was gone forever.

I also found Mazso, the girl who sat behind me in class and whom I liked very much. She had made a lovely black-and-white drawing in my memory book. When we met in Birkenau, she said to me, "After the war, when you go home, I want you to seek out my boyfriend and tell him how much I love him."

"What do you mean, I should tell him?" I asked her. "You'll go home and you'll tell him."

She looked at me with a sweet smile on her face and said, "I know you will make it, and I know I won't."

She was sixteen. How did she know that, and what did she know about me that made her think that? More importantly, why didn't we stay together? We liked each other. We could have helped each other survive. She was my good friend. Why didn't I stay with her?

All these questions I have now, with no answers.

I didn't see terrible things in my time at Auschwitz-Birkenau. I heard stories but I didn't see those things myself. I saw no one getting killed. I saw guards using their whips on people when they didn't like the way they were standing at roll call or were whispering something to the person next to them, but that was the worst thing I saw. I had no idea that there was such a thing as a crematorium or a gas chamber. When I spoke to Hedy or Mazso, we didn't talk about any of that. The one or two people in my barracks whom I spoke to didn't say anything about it either.

But why did I never ask? Maybe I just didn't know what to ask. I saw the Nazis take my father, and I saw my mother walking away. I thought they were going to another camp. Maybe if I had known that my mother was gone, that they were taking my father immediately to the crematorium, my fate would have been the same as that of my friends Hedy and Mazso. I would have just given up. What would have been the point of going on? My ignorance saved me.

11

Fallersleben

I WAS ALONE, day after day, week after week. I went to look for friends or relatives, and I found my father's brother Sandor's wife, Olga, and their daughter Marika. I tried to join them, but somehow I felt more alone when I was with them than when I was on my own. They were at the other end of the camp, and I never really went to visit them. Three months later, I found my father's brother Zoltan's wife, Margit, and her daughters, Kati and Eva. We hadn't been close at home. My mother and Margit were not friends, and even though Kati was a year older than me and Eva a year younger, we hadn't spent time together before the war.

I don't know why I went to visit them that day. I suppose I must have been feeling particularly lonely, and they were family after all. In their barracks, there were wooden bunk beds in two rows. The three of them had top bunks, and I remember standing there beside their bunks and talking to them for just a few minutes when the whistle blew and an order was given on the loudspeaker: "Immediate roll call. Stay where you are. Do not attempt to go back to your own barracks."

This was the first time we had ever heard that order, and in a minute, everyone was standing in rows of five in front of the barracks. Then a Nazi guard came and began a selection. We were marched away from the barracks and taken to the showers. We were told to shower and dress and were given a piece of bread. But then, instead of getting on the waiting train, all thousand of us were ordered to march across the road, where there was an empty area and barracks. We were then told to take off our clothes and shoes, leave them outside and go into the barracks naked. Then the guards locked the door. We were locked in that barracks, naked, for about twenty-four hours.

What we didn't know at the time was that about a thousand women had been selected, many of them to go to Fallersleben, Germany, to work in an ammunition factory for the Reich, a factory run by Volkswagen. The management of that factory needed workers immediately. But the Allies had bombed Fallersleben, and the street where the factory was had been hit. The bombs missed the factory completely but demolished the other side of the street where our dormitory was to be. The first, second and third floors of the building were in ruins. Once the rubble around the dormitory was cleared, the basement was found to be intact and the dormitory usable. If the Allies had destroyed the whole dormitory, there would have been no place for us to stay, and we would surely have been sent to the gas chambers.

The next day, the guards let us out and took us to the disinfectant area for the second time. We showered and were given shoes and a piece of bread, and were then taken to the cattle cars. There was a great mob of women being led toward the cattle cars, and I was focusing on all four of us staying together and getting into the car closest to us. But my cousin Kati was drifting away with the crowd toward another car about fifty feet away and didn't realize she was getting farther away from us. I saw that her mother and sister hadn't noticed, and I started screaming after her. It was very noisy, but I kept screaming her name and she finally heard me and looked at me. I motioned for her to come back, and she hurried back to us, so we all managed to get into the same car. That turned out to be important since we realized later that only five hundred women were sent to Fallersleben, and the cars containing the five hundred behind us was detached and sent to another place before we got there. Kati's mother would have lost her mind if she realized that Kati, her favourite child, was not with us. When we were separated, we never knew if we would see each other again, so staying together all the time was the most important thing.

I don't remember much about the train ride to Fallersleben. We had no idea where we were being taken or what would happen to us once we got there. For a lot of people, being left for a day waiting, naked, in that empty barracks, not knowing what our fate would be, was traumatic and, even though I wasn't as knowledgeable as some of the others, it was still terribly frightening. But I think we all felt some small sense of hope that maybe, just maybe, wherever we were being taken would be better than Auschwitz-Birkenau. And indeed it was.

It took about a day or two to get to Fallersleben. When we arrived, we saw the devastation of the Allied bombing, though the small village seemed to be intact, as far as we could see when we marched through it. So was the factory on the left side of the street at the edge of the village, along with a few small apartment and office buildings. But everything on the right side was in ruins, including our dormitory building.

Ironically, when we saw the effects of the Allied bombing, we didn't even dare to hope that an end to the war was in sight. We had no way of knowing how the war was going. We also had no idea about the horrors that the Nazis had inflicted on our countries, our homes and all of our loved ones. One of the terrible things about that time was our being totally in the dark, with no appreciation of what was going on elsewhere.

When we entered the dormitory at Fallersleben after being in Auschwitz, the contrast made it seem like we were arriving at a hotel. The basement was decently built—for workers, not for Jews. There were some big holes in the ceiling with exposed metal cables that supported the building, but it was clean and the floor was tiled. The area was divided into two sections, a smaller one on the left that was about a third of the total space, and the larger area, the long dormitory on the right, which contained rows and rows of two-tiered single bunk beds.

We were all thrilled to see we would have an indoor facility to sleep in and wooden bunks with mattresses, each with a blanket and a pillow.

The last row of bunks in the larger area was reserved for the makeshift hospital. One of the women declared that she was a nurse and her daughter was her assistant, so they were in charge of the hospital and didn't have to go to work. The rest of us were told to go in and claim a bed, and within moments, the beds were all filled up. We slept two to a bunk, so Kati and I claimed an upper bunk and her mother and Eva a lower one. Then we were shown into a big bathroom that had a dozen or more showers with hot water. What a luxury!

We were disinfected twice and told to shower. I still had on my old dress, but we were also given coats. My coat looked like Persian lamb, and I loved it because it smelled of someone's perfume. It smelled so good that I couldn't stop smelling it.

Then the female Nazi guards had us assemble and asked us who spoke German. One of the women, Brana, who spoke fluent Yiddish, put her hand up. She was from Huszt, in the northeastern part of Hungary, and that area had several small towns and villages where Orthodox Jews from Poland and Lithuania who were fleeing the Nazis had settled. She became the *Lagerälteste*, in charge of all the inmates, and very quickly, the smaller section of the dormitory became her domain, where she and her family, friends and neighbours lived.

At one point, I found a little gold-rimmed porcelain medal about the size of a nickel with a Star of David on one side in the bottom hem of my new coat. Obviously, it had been someone's treasure. It was so pretty, and I was happy to have found it. When I showed it to my auntie, however, she took it away from me and said we had to give it to Brana. Maybe she thought that Brana would get us an extra piece of bread or something because it was in Brana's power to do that. But I don't think we got anything; I certainly did not.

It didn't really matter because the food at Fallersleben was much better than in Birkenau. Soup was distributed to us from the same kind of barrel that was used in Auschwitz-Birkenau, but here the soup that was ladled into our bowls had a few small chunks of meat and some vegetables in it. It tasted delicious, but then, of course, anything would have tasted delicious after the horrible dirty liquid that we were used to. It was nourishing food, but it wasn't given to us out of the goodness of the Nazis' hearts. They expected us to work six days a week in twelve-hour shifts. Even on the seventh day, little groups of us were commandeered to go and do some work digging in the gardens or the fields of the nearby farms. Twenty or thirty people were picked, given shovels and forced to walk through the town to the fields to work.

When my cousin Kati was chosen to go to the fields, I thought that my aunt wished it had been me chosen instead of Kati. But perhaps I misjudged her. Maybe she only did the best she could with me, this relatively strange third person who was now with her family.

I was taken to the fields only once, and I have a memory of marching under guard through the town, in the centre of the road. The street was empty of people, and all the houses' doors and windows were closed. As we were walking, I noticed that one window of a small bungalow was open. A sheer white curtain fluttered in the breeze, in and out of the window, which had flowers on its sill, and I thought, *While this is going on with us, there are still people living normal lives, with curtains and flowers*. That billowing, sheer curtain represented everything good that we had lost.

12

Work and Hope

FOR THE FIRST few months at Fallersleben following my arrival, I worked at an assembly line. I sat at a table on which there were little trains running on a track, like children's toys. The trains carried components of some kind of ammunition, and my task was simple, like adjusting or adding something. Even though the conditions were better in Fallersleben than they had been in Birkenau, the almighty Nazi guards were always watching us, walking around in their freshly ironed uniforms and their shiny boots. I hated them and began waiting for the air-raid sirens that warned of an imminent Allied attack to go off. The sirens were wonderful diversions for me because, whenever there was an air raid, I saw fear in the female SS guards' faces.

When we were working in the factory and there was an air raid, we continued to work. But if the sirens went off at night when we were in the dormitory sleeping, the guards couldn't run fast enough to the bunkers. I loved to see human fear on their faces. It was deserved. They made us go to the bunkers too, only because they didn't want to leave us alone in case we would try to run away. I don't remember them ever beating us other than when they were in a rush to get to the bunkers during the air raids. While we were in the bunkers, some of the women would sing or recite poetry to pass the time.

Once I tried to do a bit of sabotage at that assembly line. I was hoping to slow the pace of the production of their ammunition, so I worked slower than I was supposed to. But I wasn't clever enough to tell the others what I was doing, and the guards noticed that the work was piling up behind me and there was nothing happening in front of me. I was lucky they didn't beat me when they realized what I was doing. They moved me to another job.

Now I was working at a huge pressing machine. The press was massive, maybe twelve feet high and very wide, and my work consisted of taking a metal plate from a stash and placing it on the metal cradle in front of me. Next, I had to push with my feet for the top part to come down and form the plate into a shape. Then I had to take it out of the press with my hands. The overseers warned me to take my hands out of the way when I pushed with my feet so that the top wouldn't come down and crush my hands. The work was monotonous, but I was very conscious of that advice.

The press stood close to the large double garage-like doors through which the trucks brought in supplies like metals and chemicals that were needed for the production. They opened these doors and the trucks just rolled in. It was winter by then and very cold, and when they opened the doors, the cold winter air came blasting in. The guard who stood close to me, about ten feet away, was dressed warmly in a wool uniform with a wool winter coat, hat, gloves and boots. I was wearing just my little cotton dress and no underwear. They didn't let us wear a coat when we worked, so I could only wear my coat going from the dormitory to the factory and back again. It was freezing in my little dress, and I got so cold that eventually I did something we were forbidden to do. I cut a piece from the end of the blanket on my bed and wrapped it around my body under my dress. I was skinny, so it didn't show.

At some point during our time in Fallersleben, there was a mumps epidemic, and Eva caught the mumps. I envied her because she could lie there for days without working, so when no one was looking, I would sneak into her bed and hug her, rub my face against hers and snuggle up to her in the hopes of catching the mumps. But I never did.

I did get sick once. A large boil developed under my arm. It grew and became so bad that I developed a high fever, and I started to pass in and out of consciousness because of it. I was in the "infirmary" for three days, most of the time with high fever. It was just a separated room in the dormitory. There was no medication. All the nurse and her assistant did for me was put a cold cloth on my forehead a few times. Eventually, when the boil became ripe, they cut it, and it burst open and drained. The following day, I had to go back to work. I found out much later that the lump was caused by a vitamin deficiency, but I was young and strong and lucky, and I survived.

Other than that and the mumps outbreak, I don't remember anyone getting sick. People were afraid to go to the infirmary because of our experiences at Auschwitz-Birkenau. Getting sick meant being sent away from this relatively good place and never coming back.

I kept pretty much to myself in the dormitory, even though there were about three hundred of us in the large room and about two hundred in the smaller room with Brana. I didn't really make any friends while I was there, but I remember speaking to two sisters who had the bed next to ours. There was also a young woman whom my cousin Kati knew named Maco Kranstor. She was there with her mother who had somewhat lost her mind. She did certain things that were surprising. When we had gotten off the train coming from Auschwitz and we had to walk to our dormitory, Maco's mother stopped at the side of the road and just urinated standing there. She had been a lady with a well-to-do husband and a position in society, and it was shocking to see her doing that.

Maco did everything she could for her mother. She took care of her and kept her safe. She was the smartest and the worldliest among us and knew how to get things done, like procuring extra bread and Aspirin for her mother. Maco kept her mother alive through the war. Without Maco, her mother would have been gone in a week.

Maco was probably twenty then, and I had just turned sixteen. She was mature beyond her years, and experienced, unlike me. I admired her tremendously for her devotion and for the courageous things she did. Once, she went to a Nazi guard and offered her services as a psychic. She pulled it off, and the Nazi guards started to believe in her and her special powers. She came to believe it herself too and told Kati and me that there were times when she actually thought she could channel something. She also played the accordion and sang, so she offered to entertain the Nazi guards. This put her in good standing.

During our time as bedmates in Fallersleben, I became very close with Kati. When we lay in our bunk together, we talked and got to know each other better. I started liking her more, and I think she liked me more too. I don't remember what we talked about, but I suppose we talked about what would happen after the war—if we would go back home or how and where we were going to live. We also talked about the past, about school. She had left school at the end of Grade 8 to be an apprentice and learn a trade. This is what most young Jewish women were told to do. My mother had sent me to learn sewing as well, but after picking up pins and needles from a dusty, dirty floor for one day, I'd had enough and refused to go back. Kati's mother had found a shop where they made custom lingerie, bras, slips, corsets and panties, and Kati was working there while I was still going on to Grades 9 and 10. She had also had boyfriends, while I had only started dating a few months before we were taken away.

When we came back from our shifts in the factory, Kati and I would take our showers together before we went to get our food. Especially in the winter, it was lifesaving to have the hot showers because the factory was so very cold. We had found some crystals that were being used to take rust off metals, and we used them as shampoo to wash our hair and our bodies. But we had to be careful to leave them on our skin for only a split second because they would burn a hole in our skin if we left them on any longer. We also washed our dresses under the showers with those crystals.

In the dormitory, rats walked on the cables where the ceiling had been destroyed by the Allied bombing, not far above our bunks. The rats were very big, huge actually, but we got used to seeing them there above us, coming and going. We took turns washing our dresses on Sundays when we didn't have to go to work in the factory and then hung them overnight on the metal cables to dry. Since we didn't have any underwear, we would huddle under our blankets in our bunks while they were drying.

One morning, I woke up and found that a large part of the skirt on my dress had been chewed off by the rats. What to do? Someone had a needle and thread, and we managed to repair it somehow. My skirt became quite a bit less flared, but I had something to wear and could go to work. Some things could be negotiated with the women Nazi guards, such as a needle and thread.

The work at Fallersleben was tolerable. It wasn't beyond our strength. As time went by, the soup got a little thinner and there was no more meat. The piece of bread got smaller too. We were very thin but, still, it was much better than Auschwitz.

Eventually I was apparently forgiven for my attempt at subterfuge, and was taken off the press and put at a different assembly line. Across from me at that table were male French political prisoners. We were warned not to talk to them or even look at them, and the guards watched us closely. I hardly remember what my job was, but I remember what the young man sitting across from me did since I looked at him twelve hours a day. He was given metal propellor blades with handles, and, wearing a special glove, he would twist the blades, bend them and push them into a tube that ran in front of him. The tube ran in front of me too, and I also had to put something in it, but I don't remember what it was.

It was some time in February 1945 that this young Frenchman gave us the first news about the war that we'd had since we left home in May 1944. All that time, none of us knew what was going on in the world outside. We always wondered: If we lived through this time, would there be a world when we came out? What if Hitler won?

In a moment when the guard wasn't looking, the French prisoner motioned to me and threw a tiny twisted piece of paper toward my foot. We couldn't talk—he was too far away and the factory was noisy—but when he signalled me, I picked up the piece of paper and put it in my shoe. I read it later to the women in the dormitory. It was written in French, but I could understand it because of my French classes in high school. I read the words, which I remember as if they were written today: "Don't give up hope. The Allies are advancing. It won't be long now."

When I read this bit of positive news to everyone, we felt like we had won the biggest lottery. Suddenly there was hope—hope based on facts.

Another time, the same nice French prisoner managed to send me a little paper package, which I again put in my big, clunky wooden-soled shoe. When I got back to the dormitory, I opened the package and found a Danish pastry. My auntie cut the Danish in four, and we each had a bite. A week later, I received another slim package—a toothbrush. We shared the toothbrush too.

I never had a chance to thank this young man for his kindness because, soon after, all five hundred of us were taken away. I do not know what became of him.

13
Liberation

ONE DAY, IN the spring of 1945, instead of going into the factory to work, we were shoved into cattle cars. Later I learned that we were taken east, away from the advancing Allied troops. But as the Soviets were advancing from the east, we couldn't go very far, and so we were dropped off at a little camp called Salzwedel. I still have my identification document from Salzwedel. There is no photo of me in it, just my fingerprint.

We were once again in the same kind of barracks that we had stayed in in Auschwitz-Birkenau—wooden structures with a beaten earth floor. We were surrounded by electrified barbed wire fences, and there was an armed guard at the gate. We slept lying on the ground, but at least there was a large lavatory that had actual toilets. Unfortunately, there were no showers. We were there for four or five days, and there was absolutely nothing to eat. By the fifth day, the hunger was so bad that somehow we were not feeling hungry anymore. We just lay on the ground, lethargic, weak and empty.

We were allowed to walk around outside the barracks but there was nowhere to go. One day, my auntie, Kati, Eva and I were walking around the compound, where there was a large warehouse, and we saw a panel truck drive up to the door of the warehouse and drop off a load of carrots. We wanted some of those carrots badly. It was the first food we had seen in days, and the garage door was wide open. The carrots were right there, but there was an armed guard patrolling the warehouse, walking around the building. My aunt decided that since I was the fastest, I should go inside the warehouse to steal some carrots for us. Hopefully, I could do it before the guard came around to the front again, caught me and shot me. When the guard disappeared around the side of the building, I made a run for it, grabbed two bunches of carrots, one in each hand, and ran back as fast as I could. I made it, and we feasted on those carrots. Admittedly, I later fought feelings of resentment that my aunt risked my life to feed herself and her daughters.

April 14, 1945, was a beautiful, sunny day, and Kati and I decided to go outside and soak in some sun. We sat on the ground outside with our backs against the barracks wall. We lifted our faces to the warmth of the sun. Despite the carrots, we were weak and lethargic. Then someone walked by and said, "We are liberated."

Kati and I looked at each other, and I said, "Oh, yeah. Sure."

We just continued to sit there, but then, a few minutes later, another person came by and said, "Don't you know? The Nazis are gone."

At that point, we decided it was worth standing up to go check it out. We got up and walked to where the guard had been at the gate. Lo and behold, the guard was gone, the gate was open and the place looked like a parking lot, full of American jeeps and young soldiers yelling to us, "You're free! You're free!" They were throwing us chewing gum and candies and told us to go into town and take whatever we wanted. "If anyone denies you anything," they said, "find one of us."

People were already coming back from town, their arms loaded with whole salamis, jars of jam and hunks of cheese. It was a miracle!

"Be careful," the Americans warned us. "Don't eat too much because your systems are not used to normal food anymore and you'll get sick."

I wasn't even hungry. More than anything, we wanted to take off what we had been wearing since we had arrived in Auschwitz and get clothes. Kati and I hurried back to get my aunt and Eva, and the four of us walked to the nearby town.

Some businesses were open and camp survivors were going in and out. Stores with food were particularly busy. But we were looking for a dress shop. What we found was a cleaners, and we each took a sweater. I picked out a white one. Then we found a fabric shop. There were bolts and bolts of fabric there, and we looked in awe at it all, the different designs, the flannels, wools and silks. We wanted everything. I picked out a bolt of silky material that I wanted for a skirt. It had a black background and large colourful flower petals. Then I got a second bolt of wool fabric, which I thought would be good for a coat. My auntie told us she had never sewed in her life, but she promised to sew dresses for us all and picked up a big box, filling it with thread and needles and scissors and pins. We also picked out some white material with which to make blouses and a light-blue thin checkered flannel for slips and panties. Then we started back to the camp. But all that activity had made us so tired, and we didn't have the strength to carry it all back. I dropped the bolt of wool fabric on the street halfway back to the barracks, but I held on to the black silky cloth in my arms.

It was that day, when we came back with all the fabric, the day of liberation, my happiest day, that my aunt and two cousins sat down with me and told me about my mother. They told me that the road I had seen my mother on as she walked away from me led to the gas chamber. They said they hadn't wanted to destroy my hope of ever seeing her again. That's why they hadn't told me sooner.

I had been with my aunt and her girls from August 1944 to mid-April 1945, and all that time, when they heard me talk about being reunited with my mother when it was over, they never said a word. They must have warned the people who slept around us not to tell me as well because everyone seemed to know except me. All those months had gone by, and they let me hope. It was crushing news.

My mother was not coming back, and I was devastated. I didn't want to live when I found out. I felt I couldn't. I knew I would be alone in the world now, and that was a terrible reality that I could not face.

14
The Return Home

AFTER THAT DAY, I suppose I just kept going on with daily matters — food and thinking about what we were going to do, what we could do. Those who had come back from town with sausages and jams and cheese and ate a lot, immediately got deathly ill. People lost control of their bowels, and when they tried to get to the washroom at night, they let go on the way because they didn't have the strength to hold it back. The toilets were soon overflowing, and no one could use them anymore or get to the sink because the filth was running all over the floor. The stench became unbearable, and our barracks were a nightmare. Eventually, we got help from a whole squadron of former Yugoslavian political prisoners to clean it up. They came and cleaned up those terrible toilets and bathrooms, and those of us who could did our best to clean the barracks, considering the floors were made of earth.

I got an identification document in Salzwedel, and I still have it. There is no photo of me in it, just my fingerprint.

There was more bad news on the way. I don't really know the politics of why this happened, but about a week after we were liberated by the Americans, they left and the British took over. Then, after about another week, the Soviets came and the British left. The Soviets locked us in the camp. We had to stay in those barracks for another month before we were finally released.

We had felt secure with the Americans and the British, but when the Soviets came, things were different. Before they came, we could go out to the fields and pick whatever was growing—potatoes or whatever else we could find in the earth—to supplement what the army was giving us, usually some soup and lots of bread. But the Soviets closed the gates and stationed a guard with a gun at the entrance. We couldn't go out, and they told us that if we snuck out and they saw us in the fields, they would shoot us. The war was over, and they made us prisoners again. It felt the same as it did with the Nazis, and we were very worried and scared.

Fortunately, the powers that be came to the conclusion that we could leave, and American trucks came and took us away. That was another happy moment for me. We were taken to a displaced persons camp not far from the infamous Bergen-Belsen concentration camp. For the first time since the war started, my auntie, Kati, Eva and I had a room to ourselves, though we shared with a girl whom Kati and her family knew from our town. Our room had beds with linens and there were bathrooms nearby. It was the first time since we were taken from our homes that we had what felt to us like luxurious living conditions. We were there for the next two or three months, and as she had promised, my auntie sewed for us. We each got a dress or two, white blouses, skirts and underwear.

Maco was also there and had already made connections with the officers who ran the camp. She arranged that she, Kati and I would entertain the soldiers on their day off with dances. She had taken ballet and belly dancing classes, so she was the dancer in the front and we two were in the back. "Just watch what I'm doing and do the same thing," she told us.

We must have looked a sight since Kati and I were like skeletons. Maco wasn't. She had curves, even after everything we had been through. I suppose the Germans had given her enough bread and food to keep her and her mother well fed.

Apparently our act wasn't so bad because the soldiers invited us back two or three times to perform for them. As payment, they gave us a carton of cigarettes, which was like gold at that time. It was the currency, the real wealth. We gave it to my auntie, and she went to the market, and for six cigarettes she was able to get some items we needed along with a big slab of bacon that we sliced and had on bread.

During this period, some of the young soldiers offered us rides in their jeeps. They were gentlemanly and kind. It felt amazing to be free and young and alive. One particularly tall, handsome soldier clearly stands out in my memory. He liked me. I was too scared to do anything in response other than smile back at him. He gave me a photo of a group of them, which I have to this day.

At some point, we met two Jewish young men who were three or four years older than we were and had come over to look for relatives. They were living in Hanover and invited Kati and me to visit them. We decided we would, and since there were no trains running, we hitchhiked. Eventually we got to the city and found their apartment. We spent a few nights there with them, and they behaved like gentlemen. They took us to the American Jewish Joint Distribution Committee, or "the Joint," as it was referred to, where we could get some clothes and shoes. I was still wearing the wooden-soled German clogs I had received when I arrived at Auschwitz-Birkenau. I got some boots as well as another identification card, this time with a photo. I still have that piece of identification.

Sometime in August, about three months after liberation, the time came for us to leave, and I wasn't sure what to do. I had just turned seventeen, and I didn't want to go back to my hometown with my mother and father gone. Besides, the people from the American organization that was there to support refugees (the Joint) told us that anyone who wanted to stay and wait for a visa to the United States would be looked after. My auntie, however, wanted to go home. She was still young at that time, in her mid-thirties, and she was hoping that her husband, Zoltan, would come back from the forced labour battalion. She wanted to be there when he got home and promised that if he didn't come back she would bring us back to Germany. I trusted her, and so I agreed to go back to Oradea with her and my cousins.

The Americans managed to get several railway cars together for people who had decided to return home, which ended up being a few hundred people. But they warned us that the trip itself would be dangerous because the somewhat barbaric Soviet soldiers were around. Also, there wasn't much fuel available, so the trip could take a long time.

We stopped often on that journey and waited on the side tracks, sometimes for a few days, until they could get some more fuel or a new conductor to drive the train, but we never got off the train. First of all, there was nothing to do or see, and also, we were told that the Soviets were raping women and stealing wherever they could. So when we were told that the Soviets were nearby, we managed to hide and avoid any tragedies.

In the end, it took us two weeks to make that trip from Germany to Romania. There were some cattle cars attached to the regular train cars, and for a change of scene we would sometimes go and sit at the open doors, walk around in the cars or lay down. Before we had left, my aunt was able to trade the remaining cigarettes for bacon, and we had that with us on the train. I think we were given some bread, but I don't remember where the food came from or, for that matter, being hungry.

As we got closer to home, I started getting excited about seeing my aunt Ilus again. If I couldn't have my mother, I wanted more than anything to have my Ilus néni. But I was also worried about what would happen if Ilus and Feri weren't there to welcome me to their home, the home I hoped would be mine now. Ilus had converted to Christianity, counting on that to protect her from the Nazis, but I knew that even people who had converted to Christianity were sent to Auschwitz and killed.[1]

1 Many Jews in Hungary converted after the German occupation in 1944 because the Christian churches attempted to save converts from the worst of the Nazis' anti-Jewish laws. Jewish converts to Christianity were still considered to be Jewish according to Nazi racial laws; however, some of them received protective passes that helped them survive.

My parents and I had left some of our valuables, few that they were—my memory book, photographs, my mother's brooch and ring and my precious piano—with Ilus and Feri, and I prayed those things were not gone. I was determined not to stay with my aunt Margit and her daughters. I knew I couldn't possibly live in their apartment with them—I was not invited—and I didn't know what I would do if I had no other place to go.

15
Back in Oradea

WHEN WE FINALLY arrived back home, I said goodbye to Margit and Eva and started running all the way to my aunt's house. Kati came with me. When we got to Ilus's house, I rang the bell. There was no answer. I rang it again. There was still no answer, and I started to feel very anxious about what was going to happen if they weren't there anymore. Suddenly, the window just past their apartment opened and a woman leaned out and asked, "Are you Hedy?"

"Yes," I answered.

"Your aunt and uncle told me that if the bell ever rings and they aren't at home, if you arrive, that I should tell you they are okay, that they are at your uncle's brother and his wife's house, and you should come find them."

I knew where Uncle Feri's brother lived. I said goodbye to Kati, who went home to her mother, and I started running again. I knocked on the door of the house, and I was taken to where my auntie Ilus and uncle Feri were. They were making fresh dumplings and were just about to sit down to a big chicken paprikash dinner. When they saw me, we all laughed and cried at the same time and couldn't stop hugging each other. I was happy for the first time in a long while. We had a lovely chicken paprikash and dumplings dinner together, my first postwar home-cooked meal.

After dinner, we went back to Ilus and Feri's home. It was the next best thing to finding my parents, and I felt that I was not alone. They sat me down and asked me questions about what had happened after we were taken from the ghetto. I didn't tell them the long story. It was just too hard, and I didn't want to go into details about my three months in Auschwitz and eight months in Germany. I just told them about the three days in the cattle car with my parents and then the last moments when I saw my father and mother taken away. We all cried, and they never asked me about what happened again. Then, of all things, I told Ilus I wanted to try on some of her dresses. When I came out to show them how I looked, she turned to my uncle and said, "She's still a child."

Being back in Hungary was difficult. I felt the same way about the Hungarian collaborators as I did about the German Nazis who, together, had caused the deaths of hundreds of thousands of Hungarian Jews. But I could not smear the entire Hungarian Christian nation with that hatred because of my uncle Feri. I loved my uncle, and I knew he loved me. He was just the finest human being. As far as Ilus was concerned, I knew she felt guilty for having survived when her sisters did not, and she did her best to fill the void my mother had left. I felt fortunate to have them.

At that time, there was no awareness of post-traumatic stress disorder, or PTSD. We who had survived were just expected to pick ourselves up and go on. And we did. Everyone was busy trying to build a life—study, learn, pick up the pieces where we had left off, if possible, and be teenagers as much we could. I had to decide what I was going to do with my life. If I decided to go back to school, I would have to make arrangements to leave my auntie and go to another city where there was a university. And if I were accepted, I would have to find a way to make it there on my own. I didn't want to do that, to leave the little bit of security I now had.

I definitely knew I didn't want to have anything to do with sewing, so there were two other jobs that were suggested to me. One was with a cousin who had a cosmetic salon where all kinds of creams were made and sold, and the other was with my auntie's sister-in-law doing photographic enlargement in a photographer's studio. I chose the latter, and I became an apprentice in the studio and started to work about a week after I came back to Oradea, five days a week, eight or nine hours a day. I didn't get paid anything.

I enjoyed the work, although I wasn't learning a lot. The photographers did their work, and I watched them. The only thing they taught me was a technique they called pencilling, which was a process of enlarging photos that were small, faded or torn, making them into black-and-white portraits by hand, using charcoal or sometimes doing them in colour. At that time, few people could afford cameras. If they had a wedding photo or some kind of a special family photo enlarged, this was how it was done.

I started taking English lessons in case I was able to get to America. I also took gymnastics and dance classes. I loved sports and exercise and decided that I wanted to be a dance teacher or a gym teacher. My dream as a young girl had been to be a ballerina, but I thought I was too old for that now.

I had a little money coming in at that point thanks to a Jewish man who was a cabinetmaker like my father and had survived the forced labour camps. When he came back to Oradea, he took over my father's shop. On his own, he came to my aunt and uncle and told them what he was doing and that he would pay me every month whatever he could afford for having acquired my father's shop and equipment. It was very decent of him and not expected.

I knew nothing about finances, how the world worked or anything else that was practical and useful. I had my coffee in the morning and was given a sandwich to take with me to work. When I came home, dinner was ready. Ilus had help around the house, a lady who came in every day to help her with the cooking and cleaning and to do laundry. I didn't even know how to wash my own things. I was taught nothing in my youth. Not how to cook or clean, not by my mother and not by my aunt. I don't know why. Perhaps they wanted me to do better at other things.

16

Laci and Imre

MY FIRST BOYFRIEND, Laci, had been taken from the ghetto like I was and sent to concentration camps. He survived and returned home before I did. When I came home, he came to see me and asked if we could pick up where we left off. I said yes, and we started seeing each other again. At first, we just held hands. It took three months before we kissed. After the summer, Laci left Oradea to study at the university in Marosvásárhely to become a physician. That was his dream. There was no university in Oradea, and it was the school I could have gone to had I chosen to do that. He wanted me to go also, but because of my inability to understand algebra and geometry, which would have been in the entry exam, I didn't have the confidence to try it. So, he went without me.

After Laci had been at school for a few months, I learned that he had found a new girlfriend there. Hearing that totally devastated me. I was so disappointed and angry, I told him I never wanted to see him again. A few months later, his mother wrote to me and told me that he was very ill with tuberculosis. The doctors collapsed half his lung, a common treatment at that time, and he had to stay in bed for a whole year without moving. She later wrote that he survived that year by listening to classical music concerts all day long. Laci and I started writing to each other as friends. By then I had begun dating the man who would become my husband.

I had known my future husband, Imre Bohm, from when I was in Grade 8. He was four years older than me and had studied at the Orthodox Jewish boys' school. I met him at a dance that my school had arranged with the boys' school. He had introduced himself and asked me to dance. We didn't click. At least, he certainly didn't click with me. Besides, I wasn't ready. I was fourteen then but, emotionally, only really about ten. So we danced, but that was it.

When Imre was liberated after the war, he immediately came back home to Oradea. His parents had not survived. Before the war, they'd had a knitting factory where they made cotton socks, and the factory was still there so Imre took it over. Luckily, he had returned early enough to be able to reclaim it. If he had been away as long as I was, he wouldn't have had anything left to claim. Even then, most of the machines were in ruins or had been stolen. Imre used parts from those he found, cannibalizing one to rebuild another, and managed to restore two or three machines to working order. He knew something about weaving, so that came in handy too. He was also able to get his parents' apartment back, and that's where he lived.

When I returned to Oradea, I went to see my family's old apartment once, but there was another family living there. I just wanted the wall unit my father had made. It was special to me because he had made it, but the people now living in our apartment initially refused to give it back to me. Laci helped me get it back, but unfortunately we had no place to put it in my aunt's apartment so it went into storage, where sadly, it deteriorated terribly. I didn't go to my old home again until many years later when I came back to Oradea with my adult children. I first went back to Oradea when my children were eight and ten years old, but I didn't go to the apartment. It was too big a heartache for me. I stood across the street and looked up into the windows of my old home and cried, and that was it. That was as close as I could get.

Upon restoring the knitting machines, Imre started hiring people for his little factory, and my cousin Kati went to work for him at about the same time I went to work in the photography studio. So I knew that he was home, but I was dating Laci at first. I was very much in love with Laci, and when we broke up, I didn't want to go out with anyone else. I was still angry and hurt about Laci's betrayal, and I decided that it was better not to be in love. It hurt too much.

About a year later, Imre started asking me out to a dance or to a picnic or to go up to the mountains. I respected Imre and appreciated him, and he felt the same about me, which seemed perfect at the time. Imre was a very serious person and was interested in politics. He was convinced that the Iron Curtain was going to come down soon and we would be living under a communist dictatorship. He said that it would be terrible because, if you didn't become a loud and convincing communist believer, you would have no future, and that to be involved in the Communist Party would mean spying on your friends and acquaintances. He didn't want to do that. He talked to me about us leaving together and starting a new life. He said that his uncle was going to get him a passport and visa to Argentina and that appealed to me—a fresh start.

I actually hadn't thought of leaving because I liked what I knew about communism, what I read in the books in 1946 and 1947 and what other boys I met in a Jewish club I went to were talking about. They were imagining a world where everyone was equal. Those young men, the brightest and most intelligent Jewish boys, were all communists and believers in its ideals. Imre was the only one I knew who seemed to see through it. He had belonged to a Zionist group before the war and wanted to go to Palestine like his brother had. His parents had promised him that he could follow his brother there, but they didn't let him go. Instead, they insisted he work in the factory and learn how to take care of the machinery and weave, and learn the family business.

Imre and I dated for a few months, and then he asked me to marry him. After about a year of living with Ilus and Feri, I had started worrying that I might be overstaying my welcome. Maybe it was too much for them. I guess I wasn't as secure as I would have been had I been living at home with my parents, and I thought that getting married might be a good solution for my question of what to do next. I respected Imre and cared for him, so I made the decision to marry him and start a new beginning.

My aunt and uncle approved of him and didn't try to talk me out of it. What they knew of him was that he was intelligent and had managed to rescue his parents' factory. He was running the business and making a decent living though he was still young. They wanted me to make the decision myself and so I did. In the old-fashioned way, Imre asked permission from my uncle to marry me. He told me that he would stay if I decided that's what I wanted but made it clear that he wanted to go. He urged me to go with him because he believed life was going to become very difficult under the communist regime. And he was of course right, as I learned years later.

My auntie Ilus and uncle Feri knew that we were planning on leaving, but they never talked about leaving themselves. They thought that maybe they would join us later, after we were established in a new place. But they were afraid to leave everything and take their chances in a new country. If I had thought more about it, I would have been afraid too.

17
Escape

IMRE AND I got married on December 7, 1947, in the courtyard of an Orthodox synagogue in Oradea. I was all of nineteen years old. It was a compressed and short affair. We were planning on leaving the same day. My wedding gown was on loan from an actress who was a distant relative of my auntie and my mother. The whole thing was over in half an hour. I do remember walking around my husband under the *chuppah*, the wedding canopy. My aunt and uncle were there, the rabbi, and my father's brother Erno, whose wife and child had been killed in the Holocaust. Then we went back to my aunt's apartment, where we changed into travelling clothes, picked up the suitcases that were already packed and got on the train to Budapest, where Imre was to meet up with his uncle Sandor Bohm.

Sandor had become wealthy through his black-market dealings. Imre had made quite a few runs for him, taking products from Oradea that were not available in Hungary, to Budapest, and then returning with other products to Romania that were not available there. He was able to handle the guards at the border and always carried with him a couple of bottles of liquor, which managed to get him through mostly without problems. Other times, he snuck across. Sandor was preparing to leave the country about the same time we were getting married, and he told Imre that he would be in Budapest getting passports and visas to Argentina for himself, his wife and child and for half a dozen cousins and their wives and families who lived in Hungary near the border with Romania. He said he would get papers for Imre and me as well. We just had to get to Budapest where Sandor was so that we could pick up our papers and passports.

By the time we got married, the border between Romania and Hungary was closed, and we had no papers or visas that could get us to Budapest. What to do? When Ilus and Feri had married in the early 1920s, they went on their honeymoon to Budapest, which was at that time like going to Paris, and they had passports from then. We had no money, no proper ID, and there were guards patrolling the borders with orders to shoot. Imre and I took out the photos of Ilus and Feri from their old passports, glued in our photographs, and I drew stamps on them. They would have to serve as our IDs as we made our way to the border area.

Imre's grandfather had a house and a little grocery store in a village near the border with Hungary, and we headed there. Our story, in case we were asked, was that we were on our honeymoon. Imre also arranged for a farmer in that village to be our guide for crossing the border. Imre had a couple of cousins living in villages just across the border in Hungary, where he hoped we could stay once we were safely across.

On the first night in Imre's grandfather's house, a policeman came by and asked what we were doing there. We told him our story and showed him our passports. The policeman put them in the safe in the living room and sealed it with a wax stamp. He told us he'd be back in a day or two to talk to us and give us back our passports.

When the policeman left, my enterprising husband decided that we had to leave right away, and he retrieved our passports and arranged with the guide to make our escape sooner. Since we didn't know exactly when the border guards would pass by while making their rounds, we had to be at the border hours earlier than our planned crossing time, hiding in a field in deep snow, ready to make our way across when they passed.

We knew that we wouldn't have much money for the first year or so and that we needed to take as much clothing as we could with us. Since I could only carry one suitcase, I had as many clothes on as I could fit on my body. I wore about three or four dresses with a sheepskin coat over them and a hat and a scarf. My husband carried two suitcases. One had clothes and shoes in it, and the other was full of socks from his factory.

Our guide met us and walked with us for about an hour through the snow and ice-covered fields toward the border, and then he told us to lie down and wait. It was December 8 of a very cold winter, but I was sweating from all the clothes I was wearing and the suitcase I was carrying. We lay there for at least a couple of hours without moving or talking, in which time my sweat froze my hat to my face. It was so bad that I still have a sensitive spot on my temple, and I can't stand wind or even a draft to touch that side of my face.

Finally, the border guards passed across the field and our guide signalled to us that it was time to go. We walked across the icy and snow-covered field, and we were in Hungary. We just went straight across with our suitcases into the village on the other side where one of Imre's cousins lived. We knocked on the door and asked to be let in, but they wouldn't open the door.

I don't know how we managed to get to the next cousin's house which was in another village, but we did, and they gave us sanctuary. This cousin of Imre's was a young mother with a baby who was only a few months old. She and her husband and baby were also planning on leaving for Argentina with the uncle's help.

A day or two later, Imre took the train to Budapest to meet his uncle and get our passports and visas while I stayed with the cousin and waited to hear from him. When Imre got to Budapest, he phoned Sandor, who told him to come the next morning to pick up our passports, photos and some money. But, when he got there the next day, the porter told him that his uncle had left the country an hour earlier. There were no promised passports, papers or money waiting for us. We were betrayed.

We had been so sure we would be going to Argentina. Instead we were left with nothing. Every other cousin, including the cousin I was staying with, got a passport and a visa to Argentina. As a matter of fact, they all went to Buenos Aires, where there were already three or four other cousins running a family business, and they all joined it and became very wealthy.

My husband felt terribly hurt and betrayed, beyond comprehension. To make matters worse, we had expected to be taken care of financially by this uncle and also get some money that Imre was owed by a friend. But he never got that money either. We never found out why we were left out. All I know is that it took twenty years for Imre to look at his uncle and meet him again. I don't think they talked about what had happened, even then. If they did, Imre never told me.

After a week, Imre got in touch with me and told me to get on the train and come to Budapest. He had arranged for us to stay at an apartment of another cousin, Tomi, and they gave us the maid's room. It was a tiny room, just big enough for a single bed and a night table, and it was full of bedbugs and lice. I had managed to avoid lice in Auschwitz and then got them and bedbugs in the apartment of family in Budapest. They drove me crazy, and I had to wash my hair in gasoline to kill them.

When I wrote to my auntie Ilus to say that we had arrived in Budapest and were safe, I tried to pretend I was happy, which I wasn't. I had serious doubts about whether or not I had done the right thing. But I didn't voice those doubts. I just went on pretending all was well. The future was uncertain and scary.

18
Border Crossings

I DECIDED THAT I wanted to go to Bratislava to be with my mother's sister Margit, the one who had come to warn us that the war was coming. Auntie Ilus wrote to her and sent her our wedding photo, which we hadn't even seen yet.

My husband arranged for me to be smuggled across the Czechoslovakian border, but this time, I'd be travelling with an aunt of my husband's and two other people. We were driven to the border, which was across a creek, and our driver waded across the knee-deep water, carrying us, one by one, on his back to a hut, where we spent the rest of the night.

The next morning, a car came to take us to our next destination, a town I knew as Kassa, which was in Czechoslovakia at the time (now Košice, Slovakia). We were to stay the night there and travel to Bratislava the next morning. The four of us got in, but about an hour later, the driver noticed that there was a checkpoint ahead and police were stopping cars. He collected the IDs, looked at mine and told me that it wasn't good; they would not accept it. He dropped me off along the side of the highway and told me to walk through the forest to the other side of the checkpoint, where he would pick me up. I was afraid that he wasn't going to be waiting for me there, but I had no choice. By then it was early March, almost spring, and the weather wasn't quite so bad. I managed to get to the other side of the checkpoint, and the driver was waiting for me there, as he had promised. We arrived in Kassa and went to the house of the woman who ran the mikveh, the ritual bathhouse. She was working with the driver to try to help people escape across the border.

We all slept there, and the next morning when I woke up, ready to move on, everybody was gone. They had left without me because the driver didn't trust my ID and didn't want to take any chances. Once again, I had been betrayed. I was alone, I had no money, I couldn't show my ID and I didn't speak the language. There was no telephone in the house, and I didn't know how to get in touch with my aunt or my husband.

The woman whose house I was in understood my predicament and let me stay. She gave me food so I wouldn't starve but couldn't do much else—or didn't want to do much else. She told me that if someone knocked on the door or a stranger came around, I should hide in my room. Three days went by like that, and on the third day, there was a knock on the door. I hid behind the door of my room and heard two men come in and start talking in Slovak with her. I peeked through the crack of the door, and I recognized my uncle Jozsi, my mother's brother. I hadn't seen him since I was five years old, but he looked like my mother, and I knew it was him.

Jozsi had converted to Catholicism years earlier when he married a Catholic woman, and their children had been raised as Catholics. I later learned that they had managed to stay safe during the war by digging a hiding place in a building owned by him or a friend and hiding there for months when it was very dangerous.

Jozsi had come looking for me with Etel's son, his nephew Sanyi, when Margit called them and told them that I hadn't arrived. The family started to worry because sometimes people were robbed and found murdered by the roadside, or the border police got hold of them. They began to search for me and went to the Jewish community building in Kassa and told them the story. They got the addresses of all the Jews who had come back to town and then went door to door with my wedding photo. When I saw my uncle and heard his voice, I came out and was reunited with my family.

I went back with them to Bratislava and stayed with Sanyi, his wife, Ella, and their two small boys for the first three months I was there. Then I went to stay with Margit néni and waited for Imre to come. During his five or six months in Budapest, he tried to collect the money that was owed to him and make some money in the black market. When he finally came to Bratislava, we stayed with Margit. Imre borrowed money from Margit to start a business smuggling goods from Budapest to Bratislava and then back to Budapest.

On his last trip to Budapest, Imre had about $1,000 worth of merchandise with him, which would have been a nice start for us. But he was caught at the border and put in jail. He sent a coded note to my aunt, writing that he was a Hungarian Jew in jail in Bratislava and had heard that my aunt belonged to the Joint, an organization that helped people in need, and could she possibly help him or at least come visit him?

Margit got some food together, and we went to the jail to visit my husband. We pretended that we were from the Joint and were bringing food to the prisoner, and they let us see him. We couldn't get him out though, and Imre stayed in jail for a while until, eventually, they took away his merchandise, took him back to the Hungarian border and said, "There is Hungary. Go!"

Imre hid there for a couple of hours before turning around and coming right back, finding his way to Bratislava and my aunt's apartment. I was relieved that Imre was back safe and sound, but we were still in constant danger and penniless. We still had no papers and no money. We didn't speak the language. What would we do?

Imre told us that when he had been arrested, he had with him a letter from a woman who worked for the Joint in Czechoslovakia; he was taking it to someone in Hungary. This woman had a house in Budapest that the government was going to take away from her, and she was trying to sell it without the government knowing, which was illegal.

When Imre was taken in to be questioned by the officer in charge, the guards emptied his pockets, where the letter was. But the officer was called out of the room momentarily and left everything there on the table. My husband quickly ate the letter to protect this woman.

When the woman found out what Imre had done for her, she was so grateful that she arranged for us to join a group of Hungarian orphans who were being allowed into Canada.[2] The group of orphans had already been travelling for two or three weeks, making their way to London. Our benefactor managed to get us temporary passports that allowed us to leave the country. She also got us plane tickets to London and visas to Canada. Once we had the documents and tickets, we would be able to leave the country. What a blessing this woman was.

Imre's parents had buried some gold and a diamond before the war, and he found them when he got back to Oradea. He had sent the gold to his brother, who was living in what was then Palestine with an uncle, and kept the small diamond, which would be easier to hide. Before we left Bratislava, Imre sold the diamond, and we paid Margit back what we owed her and bought something frivolous to take with us to our new life—a large crystal bowl and six small crystal bowls. I still have them today.

We took the train to Prague and arrived at the airport there, where we were thoroughly searched. Our suitcases were opened and everything was taken apart. We were not allowed to take anything valuable out of the country, and the border guards went through everything, including the little case where I kept my stationery to write letters to my auntie and uncle. They even squeezed the toothpaste out of the tube. I had a sheepskin coat and Imre had his mother's nice fox-fur collar, which was valuable in those days, and they took those things away. I had hidden my watch in a jam sandwich, and I held it and

2 In 1947, the Canadian Jewish community convinced the Canadian government to allow one thousand European Jewish children under the age of eighteen to be admitted to Canada, where they were to be supported by the Jewish community. Between 1947 and 1952, 1,123 young Jewish refugees came to Canada as part of the War Orphans Project.

pretended to eat a small bite from it, so they didn't find the watch. The search took a long time. We could hear the engines on the plane revving up as the plane got ready to take off for London, while they continued to search our things. I still remember the feeling of great anxiety that the plane would leave without us.

When we landed in London in August 1948, we caught up with the group of Hungarian orphans and were all taken to Southampton, where we boarded a beautiful ship called *Aquitania* for our journey to Canada. The ship was also taking Canadian Olympic athletes home after the London summer games in 1948. I had never seen so many tall, handsome young people in my life and wondered if all Canadians looked like that.

The crossing took several days. Imre and I hadn't told anyone we were married because we wouldn't have been allowed to be in the group of orphans if we had told the truth about our ages. Instead, we told them that we were younger than we were and were cousins. The men and women were separated, and the women, all twelve of us, slept in one big room on bunk beds. I was seasick most for of the journey and threw up a lot. I couldn't eat, even though there was a beautiful dining room with lots of space and big round tables set with white linen tablecloths and white napkins. There were white buns with butter at each table setting. But the dining room was mostly empty because most of us were seasick—except for my husband. He wasn't sick at all and loved to tell the story of how he started his dinner every evening by going from one seat to another, eating a white bun with butter at each seat until he ate his way all around at the table. Though I was mostly sick, I did manage to lead the other girls in calisthenics on the deck of the boat.

19
The New World

WE ARRIVED IN Halifax at Pier 21. There were women from a Jewish agency there, waiting for us with gifts of Coca-Cola. We hated the taste, and they were upset that we didn't like it, so they got us Orange Crush instead, which we loved. They were excited that they could make us happy with such a little thing.

Within an hour or two, we were on the train to Toronto. We had hoped they would drop us off in Montreal because Imre and I had both learned French in high school, and even though I knew a little English, my husband didn't, and we thought Montreal would be a little easier for us. We had no idea what we would do when we got to Toronto except try to find work, any kind of work.

We didn't know anyone in the city, but because we were with the under-eighteen orphan group, the Canadian Jewish Congress got us a place to live. They had a house on Harbord Street near Bathurst Street, and that is where they deposited our group. We were told we could only stay there for one month and were given a room, which six or eight of us girls shared. We were fed three meals a day and got English lessons in the mornings. While I appreciated all that, I couldn't wait to start working and my married life.

One day, an Orthodox Jewish man from Hungary named Mr. Moses came to the house because there were two sisters in the group whose names were also Moses, and he thought they might be related. It turned out they were not, but he started talking to my husband, and they discovered they had some distant relatives in common. That was enough of a connection for him to offer us two rooms on the third floor of his house on Howland Avenue to rent, as his son and daughter-in-law were moving out. It sounded good to us and we decided to move there. But first we needed jobs so that we'd have money for rent. Imre found a job as a weaving and knitting machine mechanic. Mr. Moses had a relative who had a garment factory in the garment district, on Adelaide Street, and I got a job working there. I learned how to sew hems on winter coats on a special machine. I used my first paycheque to buy *Archie* and superhero comic books, which was a way for me to learn English and about the North American culture that we were strangers in. I worked in this job for about a year and a half, but the factory was dirty, dusty and dark and the job was soulless and boring, and I hated every minute of every day of it.

Now we had jobs and could consider moving. Moses bácsi, as we called him, charged us $15 a month for the two furnished rooms on the third floor of his house, which amounted to my entire salary. There was only one bathroom for the whole house and no kitchen, so I had to cook on a hot plate in my bedroom when I had time to cook. I went to see a social worker to ask her advice, and she told me that $15 a month was too much to pay for those rooms. But here was someone who was Hungarian and who might be a distant relative, so we didn't want to go anywhere else and stayed on.

We pretended to use the second room as Imre's bedroom since we were scared to tell anyone we were married, having come with the group of orphans who were under eighteen, and Moses bácsi probably thought that I was a bad girl. He was always urging us to get married, so in January 1949, we got married again. I don't remember very much about that wedding. Moses bácsi arranged it and, again, someone lent me a dress. We had a little ceremony and then came home.

I do remember that Moses bácsi gave us a frying pan for a wedding present—our only wedding gift.

When Passover came around, we had the seder with Moses bácsi and his family. Three of his married sons were also there, and one of them invited us to his house once, but the other two didn't. No one ever asked us a single question about what we had gone through or how we were doing.

Our little group of orphans was our family, but the rest of the world was not ready for us survivors. Most people didn't know about the trauma we had experienced, or they weren't interested in knowing, and we were not eager to discuss what we had been through. I learned not to talk about any of it because, when I did, I would break down and cry uncontrollably. We were given the opportunity to speak to social workers, but the one I met with had an air of superiority over the "poor immigrants." I left in tears, feeling humiliated, and after three visits, decided never to go back. I had to go on ignoring, burying and not talking about my experiences if I wanted to survive. Most survivors did that. Moving forward and building a new and better life was my singular focus.

I had never been taught how to cook and tried to learn from Moses bácsi's wife but she was like all experienced cooks, telling me to take a little of this, mix in a little water and a little egg and then add a little of that. She might as well have been speaking another language, and I wasn't any more knowledgeable about cooking after her instruction than I had been before.

After a year of living in that apartment, we wanted very much to move on. We wanted a normal home where we could start to build a life, and I wanted a real kitchen so that I wouldn't have to go to the bathroom on the second floor to wash my dishes, let alone myself.

Three years passed, and in 1951, I got a job working in the office of Vogue Patterns, a sewing pattern company. It was a better job and somewhat of an improvement. Not that I liked office work—filing and sorting and filling orders. It wasn't interesting or challenging, and I don't know why I didn't try to get a job in photography, which I was interested in and had learned about in Oradea. Perhaps it was because I had little self-confidence.

Then we moved to an apartment on Vaughan Road. I loved that apartment, but it was even more expensive than the last one, so we had to rent out a bedroom to one of the girls from our group. It was not a very comfortable arrangement because we didn't have much privacy, but we needed the extra money to pay the rent.

One of the girls in the orphans' group gave me her Hungarian cookbook, which I still have. It was from the 1930s and had yellowing, frayed pages, but it explained everything from A to Z, even how to look for produce in the market and how to store things. Everything was explained in a way that I could follow. My husband chose a few dishes that he thought he'd like, and I learned how to cook them. He wasn't picky with food. For him, as long as I could cook a chicken soup with noodles or make a meatloaf with mashed peas and sautéed onions on the side, he was happy. Actually, the meatloaf, peas and onions became a family favourite. I also learned how to make cabbage rolls, a traditional Hungarian favourite, which were a bit more complicated, but I was the one who wanted the cabbage rolls.

Imre wasn't making much money, and at some point he quit his job in the knitting factory. He didn't want to be fixing machines in factories and didn't like working for other people. He had gotten used to being his own boss after liberation, when he had run his family's business. So he started working on commission as a door-to-door salesman for a vacuum cleaner company. One of his acquaintances told him about this job and said he could make some good money doing that. But Imre wasn't very good at being a salesman and didn't make much money, though he did say that he learned a lot.

In 1953, we decided we would move in with some acquaintances, a Hungarian Jewish couple who had a little house in Scarborough. The rent would be about half what it was at our current place. By that time, I had changed jobs again and was working in the office of the

Manulife Insurance Company on Bloor Street, calculating payments for people who were buying and financing cars. We then also bought our first car, and Manulife took the payments off my wages. I felt like a slave, working all those hours and then getting a miserable little cheque after the car payments. We still did not make enough money to pay for everything we needed.

The arrangement of living with our Hungarian acquaintances lasted for about a year. There was only one kitchen and neither of us liked sharing it. The one good thing that came out of that experience was the dog. When we had moved in, the couple got a dog. Even though I was terribly afraid of dogs, I agreed they could get one because they let me choose the puppy. I found an adorable little female German shepherd who was just old enough to be taken from her mother, and I called her Livy. She was amazingly lovable and soft, and I loved it when she licked me. By the time she was grown, she weighed fifty pounds or so, a big dog who was almost as tall as I was when she stood on her hind legs and had a head as big as mine. When I came home from work in the afternoons, she was excited to see me. I totally lost my fear of dogs because of her.

My husband quit his job as a salesman and started a business with a partner, making and selling jackets and vests. But the so-called partner had another business of his own and didn't have time for their partnership. Eventually, I got involved and ended up selling the vests. I managed to sell a lot of them, a whole month's worth of inventory in one week, but that still wasn't enough. The whole enterprise lasted about a year, and we soon ate up our reserves and were living on eggs and beans for months. Then we moved back to the city again, to a main floor apartment in a duplex on Spadina Avenue.

20
A Working Mother

THE VESTS AND jackets business wasn't the only venture my husband got into, but none of the other businesses he tried worked out either. Imre got involved with partners who didn't hold up their end of the deal, and we lost years trying to recoup the money and debt we incurred. I kept my job at Manulife, but I still don't know how we managed for those first few years.

Then, in 1954, we drove to Montreal to visit a childhood friend of Imre's, and he took us to a discount shoe store where they sold inexpensive shoes that were set out on tables. There was nothing like that in Toronto at the time. We knew nothing about the shoe business. I knew about photography, and Imre knew about knitting and weaving machines, but we thought, *How hard could this be?* It would take so little money to start up and we felt we could do it.

We put down a deposit for the rent on a small store on Spadina Avenue at Queen Street. I asked two of my relatives in the United States to lend us $500 each and promised to repay them within a year or as soon as I could. We would need $1,000 for inventory. They both came through with the money. One of those cousins was Dora, a second cousin to my mother who lived in eastern Pennsylvania. My auntie Ilus connected us. She and her husband and youngest son had come to visit me the second year we were in Canada, which was wonderful for me. They stayed in a hotel in the city because we had no room for them in our little one-room flat, and she was very sweet to me and invited me to come and visit her. The other cousin was an old bachelor, Sandor Schonbrun, who was also from my mother's side, and he and his sister had a coffee company from which they had become very wealthy.

For several months, Imre and I drove almost weekly to Montreal to buy shoes and fill our car with inventory. We would drive back to Toronto with me sitting on piles of shoes. I was determined to repay the debts as soon as I possibly could, and once we opened the store, I sent Dora and Sandor each a letter and a cheque every month for a year and a half until the debts were fully repaid.

Our shoe store, Queen Shoes, was small, but we felt we could make a living with it. I didn't really know what merchandise to buy, so I just stuck my feet into some ladies' shoes, and if I liked them, I thought other women might too. And they did. I kept my office job and helped Imre with buying inventory while he ran the store.

By the time we were in the shoe business for a year, I saw that a modest living was actually possible, that maybe this time we could have the financial security we had been desiring for so long. That's when I decided that I was ready to have children. I was twenty-seven and had been married for eight years and wanted to have children before I was thirty. We both wanted children very much. We had paid off our debts, and I felt confident enough that we could then start a family.

When I got pregnant, I was very happy to be having a baby. I kept working at Manulife. In the first few months of pregnancy, I had a difficult time with nausea. I had some cravings too, particularly for pineapple and strawberries. There was a Loblaws on Bloor Street near my work, and I would buy a box of strawberries there and eat the whole thing for lunch. But when I was six months pregnant, I got fired. It was not seemly, they told me, to be in the office with a big belly. To make matters worse, when I went to the unemployment insurance office, they told me that when you got fired you were not eligible for unemployment insurance. So, when I was six months pregnant, I started working full-time at our shoe store. Not working was simply not an option.

We bought shoes for $1 and sold them for $1.98 or bought them for $1.98 and sold them for $2.98. We didn't make much money, but it paid for the rent and food. As time went on, we branched out and started buying Italian sandals from importers and did very well with that. There was a Polish and Ukrainian immigrant population in the area of Queen and Spadina, people who had been there for decades and had their own homes. They had money to shop, and they appreciated a better looking, stylish Italian shoe.

I worked in the store until nine every night until I started having labour pains one Friday night. On Saturday morning, my husband dropped me off at the Toronto General Hospital on his way to work. I was alone with a nurse, who was sitting and reading at the other end of the room, like she was at the end of a long tunnel. Nobody came around to see me; even the doctor didn't know me. Then, on Saturday night, September 1, 1956, I finally gave birth to my daughter, Vicky. I was thrilled. I had been hoping for a girl. I couldn't imagine a little boy because there had never been any little boys in my life.

In those days, the baby didn't stay with the mother after birth. The nurses only brought her in to me for an hour a day at the most and then took her away. I don't even remember being able to nurse her. I didn't understand why, and when I asked about it, I was told that those were simply the rules. When I came home from the hospital, the apartment was dusty and dirty, so I started cleaning right away and soon developed a fever. The next day, the doctor decided I needed to rest, so I went to a post-natal facility with my baby for four or five days, and that was a very nice time for me.

I loved being a mother and having my little baby girl. I had been having nightmares for many years since the Holocaust, but they went away immediately after I had my daughter. I would have loved to stay home with her but there was no way my husband could do everything in the business alone. So, I went back to work very soon after Vicky was born. Our landlady adored Vicky, and she babysat for her while I was at work. It was wonderful to know that I could leave my baby with someone who really cared for her. I would nurse her in the mornings and then go to the store to work with my husband. At noon, I would drag myself back home and nurse her again and then go back to work till the evening. At the end of the day, we would drive home together, and I would immediately have to get dinner ready for my husband. That's what was expected in those days.

My life was devoted to my marriage and to making a living, building a future where we could have a home. We had started with nothing, a suitcase full of clothes and socks. Everything we needed had to be bought. I was consumed with working and my duties at home. In addition to working all day, almost all the household duties were up to me: taking care of the baby and the apartment, paying the bills, shopping, cooking, baking and cleaning—everything. I don't know how I did it, but I did, and we managed to solve problems as they came up.

I missed having my uncle and auntie with me, never mind a mother and a father and grandparents. Here in Canada, no one knew me from before. There was not one other person whom we were close to in Toronto. There was no one for us to rely on or learn from. We were strangers to everyone except for the group of orphans with whom we had travelled to Canada. A few from that group became our only friends.

At one point, I started taking driving lessons, and once I got my licence, I would take Vicky out after dinner a few times a week and visit my friends, the girls from the Hungarian orphans' group with whom we had come to Canada. But I was reluctant to complain to my young friends. They were four or five years younger than I was, and even though they had become our family and our only friends, they were busy with their lives and they were not parents yet. Maybe if I had been more confident, I could have opened up to them, and maybe things could have been different.

I sorely missed family and the few of my classmates or cousins that I had in Oradea so, when Vicky was nine months old, I took her to visit Dora néni in Pennsylvania for a week—my first vacation. Dora pampered us, and it was wonderful to be with her and her large family. Some years later, when my children were six and eight, the four of us drove down to visit her again. They had a factory that manufactured stuffed toys, and the children were taken to the factory and told they could have anything they wanted. They couldn't get over it. We were a frugal family with very few indulgences. The children had everything they needed but not too much beyond that. And here they were given the opportunity to pick out whatever they wanted. They each picked out several large stuffed toys. On our way home, the border patrol guard asked us to open the trunk, and when she was rummaging around in there, Vicky said to me, "Isn't this lady nosy, Mummy?" That was a happy time.

When my daughter was about a year old, I decided I didn't want her to be an only child. I wanted to have two or three children. I thought about how different my life would have been if I'd had siblings. This time, I didn't care if it was a boy or girl, I just wanted another child. My son, Ronnie, was born on August 9, 1958, and he was a sweet baby, always smiling, always happy and cooperating, from his first breath. He was loving too, and he used to hug my legs while I was washing dishes at the sink. He tells me he still remembers how safe he felt holding on to my strong legs.

By the time Ronnie was born, we had moved and were living in a larger flat on Palmerston Boulevard. We had a living room, a master bedroom, the children's bedroom, a kitchen, a sunroom and an extra room. Once we moved, we got a nanny, and she had the extra room, but we only did that for a year or two. After that, we just had babysitters.

Vicky was a beautiful child, happy as any child could be, but when Ronnie was born, she was devastated. She didn't want another child in the family and felt replaced. She cried and cried, even when I tried to soothe her and hug her. It was difficult for her and difficult for me. But she eventually became a wonderful big sister and very protective toward her little brother. She enjoyed the role, and I encouraged her.

The children went to school nearby, and when Vicky was in Grade 2 and Ronnie was going to kindergarten, I taught Vicky to take her brother to school herself. I went with them once and showed her how to cross the street with Ronnie. The next day, I told her to take him herself and I followed about half a block behind. She was so careful, holding on to his hand, looking left and right. She was very reliable and wanted to do the right thing. I trusted her and relied on her.

21
Loss and Changes

AT SOME POINT I applied for compensation from the German government, which had started paying reparations to survivors. When I was asked about my story, I kept breaking down at the point when I talked about my mother walking away from me, and I couldn't continue. The decision was that I would be compensated for psychological damage, which was the lowest amount of compensation available.

Life went on at its hectic pace. We were making a living, and the children were growing up. In 1959, we leased a shoe store at Bloor and Bathurst, near where we lived on Palmerston. It became a little gold mine. Honest Ed's was almost right next to us, and the pedestrian traffic going to Honest Ed's was an advantage. We sold our shoes at very low prices, just like the merchandise at Honest Ed's, and we had baskets of shoes outside the store which would originally have sold for $30 to $40 selling from $2.98. We did very well. The idea was not to directly compete with Honest Ed's but to sell better quality shoes at discount prices.

Vicky joined the family business when she was twenty; she wanted her own store, and we rented one for her at Bloor Street and Avenue Road. It was an exclusive store where we sold beautiful merchandise—imported shoes, leather goods, slacks, skirts, jackets, handbags and imported knitwear. Vicky and I worked together at that store for about twelve years.

Family life wasn't easy, but there were good elements. In the early 1970s, we bought a cottage because it was Imre's greatest wish to fish from his front door. He loved fishing. We had been looking for something we could afford for several years. Even though the property was very large and more than we had expected to pay, it was such a lovely place and perfect for us. As soon as I sat down in the rocking chair and looked out through the window at the heavenly sight of the lake surrounded by old pine trees, I was hooked. We spent many happy times there, and I still enjoying spending time there.

I also took up yoga, which I loved. I later took up tai chi, and I continued doing yoga and tai chi for more than half a century. It is still an important part of my life and has taught me a lot over the years.

Then, in 1992, Imre suffered an aneurysm. He was having problems with a valve in his heart and had a tendency to high blood pressure, but he was on medication. The doctors had done tests and assured him he was in good shape. On that Friday, we had been to see the specialist to get the test results from his last checkup, and the doctor told him he was fine and not to worry. The tests had all come back good; he should keep doing what he was doing. He would be fine. Two days later, an aneurysm burst and he was gone.

When Imre passed away, I wanted to shift things in my life. We still had one little store at that point, but I decided I didn't want to have the business anymore. The previous year, I hadn't been working with him in the store, except when he needed some emergency help, but I was still doing the books and the banking and the bills. I thought it would be better for me to let the store go. But my son didn't agree. During the shiva, he went into the store and worked for a day with Diana, the young lady who had been working at the store with my husband. He came back and told me it would be a mistake for me not to continue the business I had been in since before he was born.

"Even if you are not convinced it is the right thing for you, go in and try it," he told me. "Go in for a day or a week and only then decide."

He talked me into it, and after the shiva I went in to the store. It felt good to be there. I was doing what I knew how to do, and I felt useful. I decided that it would be best for me to continue. By then, I had knowledge and experience in the shoe business that few people had, and I knew how to fit a foot properly. But when I started looking deeper into our finances, I found some surprises. I realized we owed money to friends and a supplier. Our Visa bill had run up high, and we had a bank loan I wasn't aware of.

I suppose I have a streak of Margit néni in me, and I knew I had to pull in the reins in order to get rid of the high-interest loans. I made a list of our debts, and I made myself a schedule to pay them off—the highest interest loans, the Visa and bank loan, first.

We had a huge amount of stock, one whole room in the house devoted to it. I had a sale and sold all of the shoes for $1.99 a pair. And I was glad to get rid of them. I started to reduce the stock in the store as well. I ordered only the most popular merchandise, and I sent back the last shipment my husband had ordered from the factory. Luckily, we had a devoted clientele that stayed with us. Diana and I knew how to talk to customers and how to fit shoes properly, so we did well, and within two years, I paid off all the debts.

At this time, I was living in a house that I loved, which we had bought in the early 1980s. It had an open living room, a dining room with steps leading down to a large family room, a second bathroom, a small bedroom and a spacious backyard overlooking a ravine. Now, I decided to sell my beautiful big home, which also helped me repay my loans. Three months after Imre died, I moved into the condo that I am still living in today.

22

Finding Love

FIVE YEARS AFTER my husband passed away, near the end of 1996, I met Jordan Pearlson. I met him through a yoga friend who happened to be a member of Temple Sinai, where he was the founding rabbi, and she and her husband were friends of his. She told me about their friend the rabbi and wanted to introduce us. When I said it wasn't going to be a good match because I was not at all religious, they laughed and told me not to worry.

When they approached him, he said, "Well, tell her to call me." I think he was used to people running after him, but I wasn't going to be running after anyone.

They said, "Oh no, you don't know this woman. She will not call you. You call her and make a date."

He did call, and we tried to make a date, but it took us close to a year to get together. The timing was not right, and I wasn't that anxious to meet someone. We finally connected and made a date to meet with our friends at a Thai restaurant. I didn't want Jordan to think I was making too big a deal about it, so I dressed casually, in jeans and a blouse. He arrived wearing a three-piece suit and a gold chain. But I immediately felt something drawing me to him. He was shy all through lunch and sat quietly, not talking very much. My friends told me later that it was very unusual for him. They couldn't believe it because he was always talkative and joking. This was the first time they had seen him like that. And I, who normally don't carry on much of a conversation in company, felt I had to break the silence and talked quite a bit.

It took several weeks before he asked me out again, to the Park Plaza Hotel for lunch. This time, I dressed up, and he came in jeans and an old checkered flannel shirt. We had a nice lunch and he started calling me. Then I asked him to come with me to a friend's house for dinner and conversation on New Year's Eve. He came, and that's when things started getting serious between us. He told me he was going to Florida in February and asked me if would I come and visit him there. I thought about it and eventually decided to go. I stayed for about a week, and it was probably the happiest week of my life.

We became a couple, but we kept our separate homes. He had been separated from his wife for a long time and had a house where he lived with his youngest daughter, Abby. His older daughter, Nessa, lived in New York, and his son was married. For the next few years, we spent a lot of time together and went on holidays in the winter, once to Arizona and twice to Portugal. For the first time in my life, I felt completely loved and appreciated and respected.

After about six or seven years, Jordan started showing signs of Alzheimer's, and within the next few years, he deteriorated and stopped being who he had been. Occasionally, when he had old friends or other rabbis visiting him, he could briefly come back to who he had been, but that was it. It was so sad and difficult to watch someone I loved become less and less himself and turn into someone I didn't know. I think it was a saving grace that we didn't live together because sometimes I just had to run away. I sometimes thought I would go crazy if I had to sit and watch him as he was.

In 2008, Jordan fell and had to be taken to Mount Sinai Hospital. He had hit his eye in the fall and was in danger of losing it. He had also broken his wrist, and when they put his arm in a cast that was too tight, he was terribly unhappy. It was difficult to see him in such pain. Within a week, on February 19, 2008, Jordan died in the hospital. He was eighty-three.

After Jordan passed away, I missed him terribly and was very lonely. It took a long time to get back to something near normal, which meant not missing him quite as much. It was a relationship that wasn't perfect in many people's eyes and even in ours. We all have our faults and negative sides, but neither of us ever had felt the kind of love we had for each other before or had expected anything like that to happen. It was a fantastic gift of fate to allow me to have it at that late time in my life.

23
New Purpose

I HAD NEVER wanted to talk about the Holocaust. But then one day, in the early 2000s, I watched Iran's president make a speech at the United Nations (UN), and I heard him deny the Holocaust. I sat there listening and couldn't believe that this could happen in my lifetime, that someone could stand at a podium in the UN and tell the world that there was no such thing as the Holocaust, that it was all a Jewish invention, an exaggeration to gain sympathy.

At that point, I decided that I had to start speaking out. If this could happen while I was still alive, it didn't bode well for the future. I had to do what I could. I had a voice. My parents didn't. My childhood friends didn't. My cousins and so many others didn't. I had to learn to speak for them. Vicky helped by practising with me. I'd start talking about what I had gone through. Then I'd break down crying, and then we'd start over. Eventually, I learned to keep my emotions under control better while I talked about my experiences, though I am never entirely in control.

When I called the Holocaust Education Centre (now the Toronto Holocaust Museum), which had a space in the Lipa Green building, they invited me in to be interviewed by two other Holocaust survivors who volunteered at the centre. They accepted me as a speaker and gave me an appointment to come to the centre and talk to students as part of a program that brought in mostly non-Jewish students from the outskirts of Toronto. A survivor would talk to the students, and then they would be shown a documentary film about the Holocaust. Many of the students would have been required to read one or two chapters in a book about the Holocaust before they came.

The first time I spoke, Vicky sat in the audience and gave me feedback, and after that, I got a little stronger every time, especially when I saw the reactions on the faces of the students when I told my story. Some had questions for me, and sometimes a student would send me a kind email afterward. I was so touched when they did.

There have been some significant moments during my speaking career when I have felt the impact of my speaking on the listeners' lives as well as on my own. Once, after speaking to a group of high school students, I received a letter from a young man who had lost his father, a police officer, when he was only sixteen years old. He was now experiencing trauma and depression. He wrote that my talk made him realize that if I was strong enough to survive what I did and do what I was doing now, he could go on too. I met another young man who presented me with roses and told me how my talk the previous year had changed his life: he realized how precious time is and took a short leave from his dental practice to be with his young baby. These surprising moments were reminders of the power of one person to make a difference in people's lives. I was truly surprised and so very pleased that I could be such a person. I became more and more confident about what I was doing and how I was doing it, and I went from being someone who couldn't talk about the horrors of the Holocaust to someone who did it all the time.

At one point, the Holocaust Education Centre started sending me out to Catholic schools in Waterloo and Kitchener with another survivor whom I knew a little from earlier years: Bill Glied. Bill was a Holocaust educator, and he spoke to students often and was so good at it. He also went on the March of the Living, a program that brings people from around the world to Poland to teach them about the history of the Holocaust and offers tours of what is left of Auschwitz-Birkenau, then takes them to Israel.

People at the Holocaust Education Centre had started talking to me about going on the March of the Living to talk to the students. At first, I was reluctant. I never wanted to go back to Auschwitz-Birkenau. In fact, it was the very last thing in the world I wanted to do. But I allowed myself to be convinced that it was important that I go. The students needed to meet someone who had lived in those barracks and understood what that meant, someone who could say, "I was here when I was your age, and this is what they did to me."

I didn't think I was being brave. I just convinced myself that it was important to do it, as I had done when I started speaking about the Holocaust; I had to do it for those who couldn't. And going on the March of the Living to Auschwitz-Birkenau for the first time in 2010, on the anniversary of my liberation date, April 14, turned out to be a tremendous gift.

My son, Ron, joined me there for the day. He hadn't thought it was a good idea for me to return there, but he decided that if I was determined to do so, he would accompany me. He and a cousin from Budapest drove to meet me in Auschwitz on the day we marched from Auschwitz to Birkenau with a group of twelve thousand Jewish students, and we walked together. On Yom HaShoah (Holocaust Remembrance Day), I was asked to light one of the memorial lights. Imagine the scene. We were outside, where there was a big podium with memorial lights. There were loudspeakers, Israeli flags, and the former chief rabbi of Israel, Rabbi Lau, made a speech to the students about his experiences as a child in the Buchenwald concentration camp. I was there, listening to "Hatikvah," the Israeli national anthem, blaring from the loudspeakers with my son. The area of Birkenau where I had been held was behind me, and in front of me were twelve thousand young Jewish students. It was April 14, the anniversary of the day I was liberated by the Americans. I was very moved and I was crying.

The second year I went on the March of the Living, in 2011, I met Jordana Lebowitz, a student from Toronto. I gave my speech to the students about my experience in the barracks, about the hundreds of women lying there on the floor in spaces not quite as wide as a yoga mat. I talked about how we Jewish inmates were coming to Auschwitz-Birkenau so fast that they couldn't finish the buildings quickly enough, and many of the barracks didn't have bunk structures. When I finished my talk, the students were asked to leave and go on to the next station. Everyone left except for one girl who was huddled over and crying in a corner. I went over to her and hugged her. That's how I met Jordana. We walked for a little while and talked. Her grandparents were Holocaust survivors. After the March of the Living was over, we kept in touch.

A few years later, when she was at Guelph University, Jordana organized the Yom HaShoah ceremony on campus and asked me to come speak. I said that of course I would. Then Jordana managed to get a cattle car shipped to the university, with the intention of showing it to her fellow students, some of whom had never even heard of Auschwitz or the Holocaust. She got permission to place it in the middle of the campus and opened it up to all the students to come inside, where she had put up some posters and photographs and stories with historical background. When I did my talk in front of the cattle car, there were around 1,200 students there.

Later, Jordana developed the cattle car into a travelling Holocaust exhibit with immersive, multimedia presentations and called it *ShadowLight*. Students would visit the exhibit and then listen to a talk about the Holocaust. A few years ago, I travelled with the exhibit to North and South Carolina and then to Georgia and Florida. It was a rewarding experience.

I always talk to the students about the power of one person. Jordana was one young woman, and she was able to make a big impact.

24
The Trials

ONE DAY IN 2014, I received a phone call from Judge Thomas Walther, a retired German lawyer and judge, and a former federal prosecutor for the Central Office of the State Justice Administrations for the Investigation of National Socialist Crimes. He was calling from Germany to ask me to come to be a witness at the trial of Oskar Gröning, who had been a bookkeeper in Auschwitz. Judge Walther had the opinion that Gröning had willingly held a job in the Nazi system designed entirely to kill humans, and so he should be held accountable as an accessory to those murders. The trial was the result of many years of work by Judge Walther to bring Gröning to justice. Over the phone, Judge Walther told me that he was prosecuting Gröning and the trial date was already set. He had seen a talk I gave on YouTube and realized I had been in Auschwitz at the same time Gröning was. So, would I come to be a witness? He was also getting in touch with Bill Glied, Max Eisen and other survivors who had been at Auschwitz at that time, trying to bring survivors to Germany to be witnesses at the trial.

By his own admission, Gröning had been an accountant in Auschwitz and had even given an interview to one of the biggest German magazines in which he described his role in Auschwitz in detail. Before people were taken to the gas chambers, they had to shed their clothes and belongings, and there was a whole crew of prisoners, known as the Kanada *Kommando*, who went through every item to look for gold and other valuables. They had to bring the money they found to Gröning, who would then either have it sent or deliver it himself to the Nazi authorities in Berlin.

Gröning had not been tried at the Nuremberg Trials. The Nuremberg Trials didn't even touch 1 per cent of the Nazis who were involved. How many innocent souls were killed and those responsible couldn't be brought to justice?

In September 2014, Gröning was charged by state prosecutors with 300,000 counts of accessory to murder, related to a period between May and July 1944, when around 425,000 Jews from Hungary were brought to the Auschwitz-Birkenau complex and most were immediately gassed to death. According to the law, he was now able to be held accountable even though he hadn't been seen to murder anyone directly. He was held accountable as a person without whom the Nazis couldn't have done what they did. Without the bakers, seamstresses, cooks, cleaners and bookkeepers, everyone who made the wheels turn, the entire system couldn't have functioned. Those drivers who brought the Zyklon B gas to the camp didn't murder anyone, but they made it possible for others to murder a great many people. Gröning admitted to being at Auschwitz and bragged about the camaraderie among the men, but he accepted no moral responsibility for his work. Gröning denied he had committed any crimes.

At first, my response to Judge Walther asking me to attend the trial was no, the same as my first reaction to speaking about the Holocaust and going on the March of the Living. How could I go back and be surrounded by the German language and by Germans in Germany? All I could think of was what they had done in Auschwitz, and to hear it all again would be horrible. No, I couldn't. But Judge Walther called again a few times and explained why my presence at the trial would be important. He finally wore me down. And he was right to do so. I knew I had a voice and others didn't. I had to go. And so, I did. Vicky came with me, bless her.

The trial had to be conducted in Lüneburg, Germany, because Gröning lived near there, and according to the law, he was entitled to be tried there. The trial started on April 20, 2015, and took three months. There was always a nurse and an ambulance waiting when Gröning was testifying, and he could only be questioned for three hours a few times a week and only in the mornings. The court was careful and gentle with Gröning during his trial because he was ninety-three years old, and they didn't want him to get ill or overtired.

We had the chance to hear the accused as well as the accusers—dozens of Holocaust survivors from across the world—and it was unbelievable to listen to Gröning tell us what a wonderful time he had in Auschwitz. They were the best years of his life, he said. He had made friends for life. They had plenty of good food and drinks, sports clubs and other activities together, and it was great fun. He didn't admit to anything except being an accountant, but eventually, he did admit to being on the ramp once or twice when the Hungarian Jews arrived in the cattle cars. There he witnessed a Nazi officer grabbing a Jewish baby by the heels and smashing the baby's head into the side of a railcar.

I have a photo of people pouring out of the cattle cars, and there is a Nazi there too in a spic and span uniform and shiny boots. It could have been him. Would I have known? Was I looking at faces then? Even if I did, I wouldn't have recognized him. I do remember shiny boots though. We were so dirty and so tired, so miserable and scared out of our minds when we poured out of those cattle cars. Then we were confronted by soldiers all shiny and clean, a contrast to our misery.

It was bewildering to listen to a Nazi, one of those whom we had so feared and hated, telling us about the good times he had in Auschwitz and how he had never hurt anyone. Strangely, I didn't really feel hatred as I listened. It was a wonder to me that he could see Auschwitz in that light and feel that way about his time there and his role in it all. If he really felt as innocent as he said he did, he couldn't have seen what was happening in Auschwitz, the corpses or the crematoria or the suffering. Or if he did see corpses, maybe he turned away because he didn't want to see them, or he pretended it had nothing to do with him. How could that be?

I reminded myself that he had grown up in a Nazi family. He was brainwashed in school, and he was sent to a Hitler Youth group where he heard nothing but how despicable and horrible the Jews were and how the world would be a better place without them. And he came to believe it, as so many others like him did. The next step was inevitable—to join the SS. It was one step at a time until the nation was filled with Nazis. They were taught to fear us, to hate us, to look down on us. We were not human in their eyes; we were not worthy to breathe the air. We were like bugs that had to be stepped on, not human beings.

On July 15, 2015, Gröning was found guilty of being an accessory to the murder of at least three hundred thousand Jews. After that trial, the judges and lawyers and the community met, television cameras everywhere. One of the survivors who was there to give testimony was Eva Mozes Kor. She and her twin sister had been part of the group of hundreds of twins upon whom Josef Mengele had conducted horrific experiments. At the end of her testimony, with television cameras all around, she went up to Gröning, hugged him and said, "I forgive you." She hugged him close, and he hugged her back.

I felt sick about it. When it was my turn to speak, I made a point at the end of my talk to say, "I cannot forgive. I cannot forgive you for murdering my parents. I don't believe I have the right to forgive you for murdering all those babies and young children. Maybe, maybe I could forgive you for what you did to me. But not what you did to all those innocents."

When I finished, I said that being in Germany, in a German court, as a witness was difficult, but I was grateful for it.

In that moment, I felt like I was putting a bouquet of flowers on my parents' non-existent graves. I was proud that I could speak when my mother couldn't, when my family couldn't. I was there to speak for them.

Gröning was sentenced to four years' imprisonment. His lawyers appealed the decision, and on November 28, 2016, there was another trial, which I attended, and he was judged to be fit for prison. During both trials, I was waiting to hear him say "I'm sorry" just once. I thought my parents should get that, at the very least. And, actually, at his second trial, he did say he was sorry during his speech, but he didn't stop there. He went on qualifying and qualifying and qualifying, until the "I'm sorry" meant nothing at all.

In the end, Gröning died on March 9, 2018, in hospital before being sent to jail.

In June 2016, I attended another trial in Germany as a witness. This one was held in Detmold, Germany, and was for the Nazi guard Reinhold Hanning. This time, there were only female judges, and I could see tears in their eyes when they listened to our testimonies. Hanning was accused of being an accessory to at least 170,000 murders. The judges eventually delivered a guilty verdict and sentenced him to five years in prison. As I gave my witness testimony, he sat with his head hanging down, looking at the ground, not looking at me. At the end of my testimony, I addressed him directly. I told him not to be afraid to look at me, that I was just another human being. Then his lawyer said something to him, and he lifted his head and looked at me with innocent blue eyes. Then he lowered his head again without speaking a word.

The hardest thing I've ever done was to get over my fears, and that led me to wonderful gifts. Talking to students about the Holocaust led me to back to Auschwitz, where I hadn't wanted to go, and that led me to act as a witness in trials in Germany, which I hadn't wanted to do. Both times, I was given gifts that I couldn't have imagined. In Germany, my gift was completely losing the fear and the hate and the resentment of Germans and the German language. This was possible because of Judge Thomas Walther and his colleagues, who worked so tirelessly to bring these criminals to justice.

I lost that dark, heavy something in me when I thought of Germany or Germans. It just evaporated. Many Germans were very kind to me.

I can now see that they are human beings like us, like me. I certainly don't hold the children and grandchildren responsible for what others did. If I did, I wouldn't be any better than the Nazis. Without wanting or realizing it, the heaviness just lifted when I was there with the nicest, kindest Germans who were working to find justice for what was done to us.

That was after decades of fear. It is always fear at the base. To get rid of that, to be free of it, is a great gift.

Epilogue

WE TALK ABOUT kindness but we often don't practise it. If I were a magician, or a person gifted by God, I would switch just one little thing in human DNA—that one tiny molecule that makes people hate to one that makes people be kind. All the religions speak about doing unto others as we would want done unto ourselves, and yet look at the history we have. Murder, pillage, pogroms, tortures. If not in every generation, then in every second one. Over and over again. Against the Jews as well as many other people. But we seem to have experienced this suffering from the beginning of our history, and it seems to be never-ending. We are robbed, we are thrown out of our homes, our countries, we are tortured, we are killed. We establish ourselves, renew ourselves, then sooner or later, it starts all over again. And what will happen now, only God knows.

I try to tell the students I speak to how important it is to be kind. I also tell them how important it is for them to trust in themselves and work for the greater good. They each can make a difference. Everyone has something special to offer. I urge them not to allow anyone to tell them that they can't or shouldn't reach for their dreams or hopes. They should not allow anyone to tell them they are not clever enough or talented enough. If they think and believe in something, they must follow their dreams and not let anyone stop them.

Before I got involved in Holocaust education, I was afraid and didn't believe I could make a difference. Then, when I started talking to students in 2002, it became a motivational force in my life. Ever since then, I have been committed to it, and it means the world to me to still be able to do it. I started very late in my life because before that I just pushed down my feelings and didn't want to talk about what I'd experienced. I felt I couldn't. But eventually, I had to, and now it is my life's purpose.

I want to feel at the end of my life that I did something to help, that I made some kind of contribution to making the world just a teensy little bit better. Even if just one person will hear my story and say: "It's true. This did happen to these people. It shouldn't happen again." That will be the fulfillment of my life's dream.

We are fortunate that we have the ability to do something. Maybe, just maybe, there is a chance for humanity.

Photographs

1 Hedy's maternal great-grandmother, Regina Grünstein Breuer. Nagyvárad, Kingdom of Hungary (now Oradea, Romania), 1860.

2 Hedy's maternal great-grandfather, Joseph Breuer. Nagyvárad, 1860.

3 Hedy's maternal grandparents, David and Berta Breuer, on their wedding day. Place unknown, circa 1889.

4 Hedy's mother (left) and aunt Ilus. Place unknown, circa 1920.

1

2

3

1 Hedy's parents, Erzsebet Breuer and Ignac Klein, on their wedding day. Place unknown, circa 1923.

2 Hedy's aunt Helen Breuer. Oradea, circa 1930.

3 Hedy with her parents. Oradea, 1928.

1

2

3

4

1 Hedy and her mother. Oradea, circa 1932.

2 Hedy's aunt Margit. Place unknown, 1935.

3 Hedy in her school uniform. Oradea, 1939.

4 Hedy and her parents. Oradea, circa 1940.

1

2

1 Hedy (standing on the far right) with cousins and friends at a beach on the Körös River. Oradea, circa 1936.

2 Hedy's class photo. Hedy is sitting in the third row from the top, fourth from the right. Oradea, circa 1939.

Hedikémnek sok szeretettel
Ne bántsa lelkedet nagy remények vágya,
Nem a jólétben van szívünk boldogsága.
Örömet nyujthat a kunyhó is, eleget,
Csak sorsával legyen a szív elégedett.
Ne csüggedjél soha megsegít az Isten,
Keress vigasztalást, enyhülést, a hitben.
Az ég angyali ide lenn is járnak
Maradjál te az én kedves Hédiskámnak
1939. szep 5. Anyuskád

An inscription in Hedy's memory book from her mother reads:

Hedy, with lots of love.

Don't let your soul be troubled by great expectations. It is not in wealth that our heart's desires reside. Even in a hovel you can live content and well, only that your heart should be content with your fate. Don't ever give up. God will help you. Find solace in faith. Angels from heaven walk here with us too. Remain always my darling Hedy.

Mom

September 5, 1939

(Translation by Hedy and her daughter, Vicky.)

A drawing and inscription in Hedy's memory book by her friend Mazso (Anna Silberman). The inscription reads:

> *The Gate of Happiness. This is where all the prayers fly. Yours should fly here too, and never find the door closed. That is my wish.*
>
> *With love, your classmate,*
>
> *Silberman, Anna*

(Translation by Hedy and Vicky.)

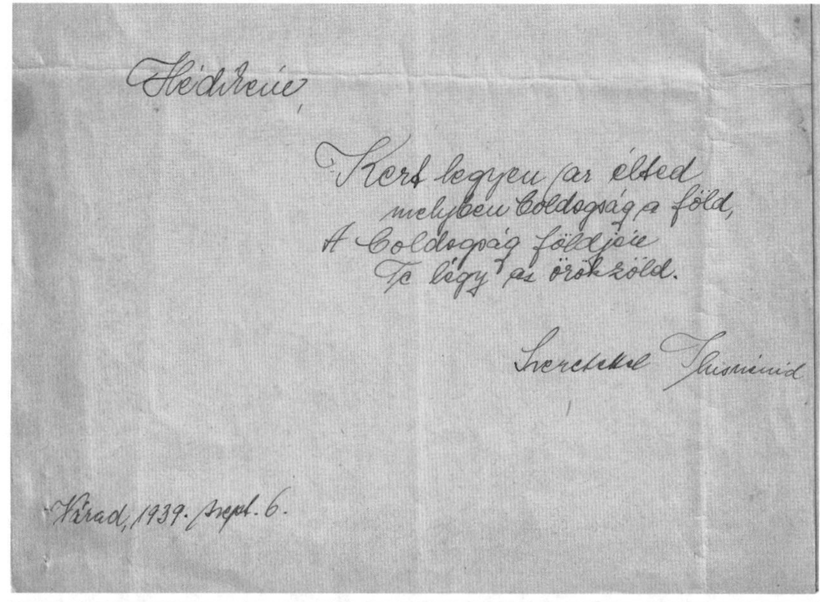

Hédikém,

Kert legyen az élted
melyben boldogság a föld,
A boldogság földjén
Te légy az örökzöld.

Szeretettel Ilusnénid

Várad, 1939. szept. 6.

An inscription in Hedy's memory book by her aunt Ilus: ***Let your life be a garden where happiness is the earth and you will be the evergreen.***

(Translation by Hedy and Vicky.)

1 2 3 4

1–4 **Pages from Hedy's memory book.**

Hedy. Oradea, 1942.

1

2

3

1 Hedy in a school performance. Left to right: Name unknown, Eva Benedek, Eva Berger, René Gantz, Hedy, Erzsok London. Oradea, circa 1942.

2 Hedy (left) with her friend Hedy Neumann. Oradea, circa 1943.

3 Hedy (right) with her friend Hedy Neumann. Oradea, circa 1943.

LEGITIMATION
to replace Identity Documents destroyed at
Concentration Camps

Name (Nom) Klein Hedwig
Birthplace (né (e) à) Oradea-Mare 1928 V.11
Country (pays) Romănie
Citizen (citoyen (ne)) Român
Where taken from? (d'où était pris (e) Oradea-Mare
In which camp (s) lived? (dans quel (s) Lager (s) vivait ?) Auschwitz
Fallersleben, Salzwedel
Prisoner from 1944 V. 29 to 1945 IV. 14
Prisonnier de jusqu' à
R.H. THUMB PRINT
Owner's signature (signature de possesseur) Klein Hedwig
Witnesses' signature (signatures des témoins) Klein Eva

1

Hannover, den 18.8.1945

Bescheinigung

Wir bescheinigen hiermit, daß der ehemalige Konzentrations-Häftling
Frau Klein, Hedwig
geb. am: 11.5.1928
bei uns ordnungsgemäß registriert worden ist.

Certification

We certify, that
Mr./Mrs. Klein, Hedwig
was concentrations-prisoner.
He/she is duly registred in our office.

2

1 Hedy's postwar identity document, issued in Salzwedel, Germany, 1945.

2 Hedy's postwar identity document, issued in Hanover, Germany, 1945.

1

2

1 Hedy (left) and her cousins Eva and Kati in the dresses her aunt Margit sewed for them after the war. Near the Bergen-Belsen displaced persons camp, Germany, 1945.

2 Hedy and her first boyfriend, Laci. Oradea, 1945.

1

2

3

1 Hedy. Oradea, 1946.

2 Hedy and Imre on their wedding day. Oradea, December 7, 1947.

3 With the group of Hungarian orphans on the *Aquitania*. Hedy is sitting in the front, on the right. August 1948.

1

2

1 Hedy with Imre and friends from the group of Hungarian orphans. Niagara Falls, Ontario, 1948.

2 Hedy and Imre at Niagara Falls, 1948.

1

2

1 Hedy's aunt Ilus and uncle Feri. Oradea, 1949.

2 Hedy and Imre. Toronto, 1950.

1

2

3

1 Hedy. Toronto, 1955.

2 Hedy and her daughter, Vicky. Toronto, 1956.

3 Hedy and Vicky. Toronto, 1956.

1

2

3

1 Imre, Ron and Vicky. Toronto, 1963.

2 Hedy at a friend's cottage near Huntsville, Ontario. 1963.

3 Hedy and Imre in the first home they bought. Toronto, 1964.

1

2

1 Hedy with Ilus and Feri, Vicky and Ron. Oradea, 1967.

2 Vicky, Imre and Ron on the occasion of Ron's bar mitzvah. Toronto, 1971.

1

2

3

1 Hedy in her shoe store. Toronto, circa 1995.

2 Hedy and Vicky. Monterey, California, 1999.

3 Hedy with her grandsons, Joey and James. Toronto, circa 2005.

1

2

1 Hedy and Jordan Pearlson. Toronto, circa 1998.

2 Hedy with her son, Ron, while on March of the Living. Auschwitz-Birkenau State Museum, Poland, 2010.

1

2

3

1 Hedy (seated front and left) with Judge Thomas Walther (kneeling in front) and other Holocaust survivors and their families at the trial of Oskar Gröning. Lüneburg, Germany, 2015.

2 Hedy with Judge Thomas Walther. Toronto, 2105.

3 Hedy in the Volkswagen factory where she was held as a forced labourer in the Fallersleben concentration camp at the end of the war. Wolfsburg, Germany, 2016.

Hedy. Toronto, 2025.

Glossary

Allies The coalition of countries that fought against the Axis powers (Germany, Italy and Japan, and later others). At the beginning of World War II in September 1939, the coalition included France, Poland and Britain. After Germany invaded the Soviet Union in June 1941 and the United States entered the war following the bombing of Pearl Harbor by Japan on December 7, 1941, the main leaders of the Allied powers became Britain, the USSR and the United States. Other Allies included Canada, Australia, India, Greece, Mexico, Brazil, South Africa and China.

American Jewish Joint Distribution Committee (JDC) Colloquially known as the Joint, the JDC was a charitable organization founded in 1914 to provide humanitarian assistance and relief to Jews all over the world in times of crisis. It provided material support for persecuted Jews in Germany and other Nazi-occupied territories and facilitated their immigration to neutral countries such as Portugal and Turkey. Between 1939 and 1944, Joint officials helped close to 81,000 European Jews find asylum in various parts of the world. Between 1944 and 1947, the JDC assisted more than 100,000 refugees living in displaced persons camps by offering retraining programs, cultural activities and financial assistance for emigration.

Auschwitz (German; in Polish, Oświęcim) A Nazi concentration camp complex in German-occupied Poland about fifty kilometres from

Krakow, on the outskirts of the town of Oświęcim, built between 1940 and 1942. The largest camp complex established by the Nazis, Auschwitz contained three main camps: Auschwitz I, a concentration camp; Auschwitz II (Birkenau), a death camp that used gas chambers to commit mass murder; and Auschwitz III (also called Monowitz or Buna), which provided slave labour for an industrial complex. In 1942, the Nazis began to deport Jews from almost every country in Europe to Auschwitz-Birkenau, where they were selected for slave labour or for death in the gas chambers. Starting in May 1944, over 420,000 Hungarian Jews were deported to Auschwitz-Birkenau in mass transports, with smaller groups arriving through October 1944. The majority of these Jews were killed immediately in the gas chambers. In mid-January 1945, close to 60,000 inmates were sent on a death march, leaving behind only a few thousand inmates who were liberated by the Soviet army on January 27, 1945. It is estimated that 1.1 million people were murdered in Auschwitz, approximately 90 per cent of whom were Jewish; other victims included Polish prisoners, Roma and Soviet prisoners of war.

Auschwitz-Birkenau *See* Auschwitz; Birkenau.

Birkenau Also known as Auschwitz II. One of the camps in the Auschwitz complex in German-occupied Poland and the largest death camp established by the Nazis. Birkenau was built in 1941, and in 1942 the Nazis designated it as a killing centre, using Zyklon B gas to carry out the systematic murder of Jews and other people considered "undesirable" by the Nazis. In 1943, the Nazis began to use four crematoria with gas chambers that could hold up to 2,000 people each to murder the large numbers of Jews who were being brought to the camp from across Europe. Upon arrival, prisoners were selected for slave labour or sent to the gas chambers. The camp was liberated in January 1945 by the Soviet army. An estimated 1.1 million people were killed in the Auschwitz camp complex, most of them in Birkenau and the vast majority of them Jews.

black market An illegal and informal economic system that arises, often in wartime, due to shortages or government control of goods.

British Mandate Palestine (also Mandatory Palestine) The area of the Middle East under British rule from 1923 to 1948 comprising present-day Israel, Jordan, the West Bank and the Gaza Strip. The Mandate was established by the League of Nations after World War I and the collapse of the Ottoman Empire; the area was given to the British to administer until a Jewish national home could be established. During this time, Jewish immigration was severely restricted, and Jews and Arabs clashed with the British and each other as they struggled to realize their national interests. The Mandate ended on May 15, 1948, after the United Nations Partition Plan for Palestine was adopted and on the same day that the State of Israel was declared.

Canadian Jewish Congress (CJC) An advocacy organization and lobbying group for the Canadian Jewish community from 1919 to 2011 that was instrumental in the War Orphans Project. In 1947, the CJC convinced the Canadian government to allow 1,000 European Jewish children under the age of eighteen to be admitted to Canada, where they were to be supported by the Jewish community. The CJC searched for Jewish war orphans with the help of the United Nations Relief and Rehabilitation Administration (UNRRA). Between 1947 and 1952, 1,123 young Jewish refugees came to Canada. The CJC was restructured in 2007 and its functions subsumed under the Centre for Israel and Jewish Affairs (CIJA) in 2011.

cattle cars Freight cars used to deport Jews by rail to concentration camps and death camps. The European railways played a key logistical role in how the Nazis were able to transport millions of Jews from around Europe to killing centres in occupied Poland under the guise of "resettlement." The train cars were usually ten metres long and often crammed with more than a hundred people in abhorrent conditions with no water, food or sanitation. Many Jews, already weak from poor living conditions, died in the train cars from suffocation or illness before ever arriving at the camps.

communist Based on the principles of communism, a political and economic theory advocating public ownership and shared control over a society's resources. Communism was rooted in the socialist writings of nineteenth-century philosopher and economist Karl Marx (1818–1883). In the twentieth century, several countries, including the Soviet Union, China, Korea and Vietnam, adopted totalitarian communist political structures that were characterized by oppression of opposition and state-control of property and resources.

crematorium (plural, crematoria) A building where corpses are burned. The Nazis used crematoria to burn the bodies of Jews and other prisoners they murdered in concentration camps, as well as in the Auschwitz-Birkenau death camp, where the crematoria also housed gas chambers.

displaced persons camps Facilities set up by the Allied authorities and the United Nations Relief and Rehabilitation Administration (UNRRA) in October 1945 to resolve the refugee crisis that arose at the end of World War II. The camps provided temporary shelter and assistance to the millions of people who had been displaced from their home countries as a result of the war and helped them prepare for resettlement.

Fallersleben A concentration camp in Fallersleben (now Wolfsburg), Germany, that was a subcamp of the Neuengamme concentration camp. The camp was established as a men's camp in June 1944 for armaments production at a Volkswagen factory. In August 1944, a group of 500 Hungarian women were transferred to Fallersleben from Auschwitz-Birkenau, and later transports brought women from the Bergen-Belsen concentration camp, establishing it as a women's camp. Female inmates performed slave labour in the Volkswagen factory, manufacturing weapons on assembly lines. On April 7, 1945, surviving female inmates were evacuated to the Salzwedel subcamp. *See also* Auschwitz; Salzwedel.

forced labour battalions (Also referred to as Auxiliary Labour Service or forced labour service) Units of Hungary's military-related labour service system (in Hungarian, Munkaszolgálat), which was first established in 1919 for those considered too "politically unreliable" for regular military service. After the labour service was made compulsory in 1939, Jewish men of military age were recruited to serve; however, having been deemed "unfit" to bear arms, they were equipped with tools and employed in mining, road and rail construction and maintenance work. Though the men were treated relatively well at first, the system became increasingly punitive. By 1941, Jews in forced labour battalions were required to wear an armband and civilian clothes; they had no formal rank and were unarmed; they were often mistreated by extremely antisemitic supervisors; and the work they had to do, such as clearing minefields, was often fatal. By 1942, 100,000 Jewish men had been drafted into labour battalions, and by the time the Germans occupied Hungary in March 1944, between 25,000 and 40,000 Hungarian Jewish men had died during their forced labour service.

gas chamber A sealed room into which either carbon monoxide or Zyklon B, a poisonous gas, was emitted in order to kill people. The Nazis began experimenting with carbon monoxide gas in late 1939, using it to kill people with mental or physical disabilities. In mid-1941, they began using gas vans, sealed trucks that were filled with engine exhaust. Later that same year, the Nazis opened the first killing centre, Chelmno, in Poland, which used gas vans. Beginning in 1942, gas chambers were used at the killing centres of Belzec, Sobibor, Treblinka and Auschwitz. Smaller gas chambers were built at several concentration camps, including Stutthof, Mauthausen, Sachsenhausen and Ravensbrück.

gendarmes (derived from French, *gens d'armes*, people of arms) Members of a military or paramilitary force, or gendarmerie, in France and, during World War II, in Hungary. In Hungary, the gendarmerie carried out the Nazi regime's anti-Jewish policies, including rounding the Jews up into ghettos and deporting them to death camps.

ghetto A confined residential area for Jews. The term originated in Venice, Italy, in 1516 with a law requiring all Jews to live on a segregated, gated island known as Ghetto Nuovo. Throughout the Middle Ages in Europe, Jews were often forcibly confined to gated Jewish neighbourhoods. Beginning in 1939, the Nazis forced Jews to live in crowded and unsanitary conditions in designated areas—usually the poorest ones—of cities and towns in Eastern Europe. Ghettos were often enclosed by walls and gates, and entry and exit from the ghettos were strictly controlled. Family and community life continued to some degree, but starvation and disease were rampant. Starting in 1941, the ghettos were liquidated, and Jews were deported to camps and killing centres.

Hanning, Reinhold An SS guard at the Auschwitz concentration camp who led Jewish prisoners from the trains to the gas chambers. In 2016, Hanning was convicted in a German court as an accessory to 170,000 murders and was sentenced to five years in prison. He died in 2017 at the age of ninety-five before he served time. *See also* Auschwitz; gas chamber.

Hitler Youth (in German, Hitlerjugend [HJ]) An organization founded in the 1920s to mobilize teenage boys and indoctrinate them in Nazi ideology. A parallel organization, the League of German Girls (Bund Deutscher Mädel), was also created, and both organizations had junior branches for younger children. The Nazis banned all other youth groups in Germany, and by 1939 it became compulsory for German youth aged ten to eighteen to join these Nazi organizations. In the later years of the war, Hitler Youth were increasingly used for military purposes, such as manning anti-aircraft guns.

Iron Curtain A term made famous by former British prime minister Winston Churchill in 1946 that described the political and ideological barrier maintained by the Soviet Union to isolate its dependent allies in Eastern and Central Europe from non-Communist Western Europe after World War II. The Communist governments behind the Iron Curtain exerted rigid control over the flow of information and people to and from the West until the collapse of Communism in 1989.

Kanada *Kommando* The prisoner work detail in Auschwitz-Birkenau that worked in the Kanada warehouse sorting through the belongings and clothing that was confiscated from newly arrived prisoners. The name was adopted by the prisoners based on their belief that Canada was a land of wealth.

March of the Living An annual two-week program that takes place in Poland and Israel and aims to educate primarily Jewish students and young adults from around the world about the Holocaust and Jewish life before and during World War II. On Holocaust Memorial Day (Yom HaShoah), participants and Holocaust survivors march the three kilometres from Auschwitz to Birkenau to commemorate and honour all who perished in the Holocaust. Afterward, participants travel to Israel and join in celebrations there for Israel's remembrance and independence days. *See also* Auschwitz; Birkenau; Yom HaShoah.

Nuremberg Trials A series of war crimes trials held in Nuremberg, Germany, from November 21, 1945, to October 1, 1946, that tried twenty-two high-level Nazi officials at the first international court. Among the charges laid against the defendants was the charge of crimes against humanity, which included "murder, extermination, enslavement, deportation … and persecution on political, racial, or religious grounds." Twelve defendants, those directly involved in killing, were sentenced to death. The International Military Tribunal that adjudicated the trials, composed of judges from the four Allied powers, set important precedents in international criminal law. Twelve subsequent war crimes trials, including the I.G. Farben Trial, were held in front of military tribunals in Nuremberg between 1946 and 1949.

Orthodox (Judaism) The religious practice of Jews for whom the observance of Judaism is rooted in the traditional rabbinical interpretations of the biblical commandments. Orthodox Jewish practice is characterized by strict observance of Jewish law and tradition, such as the prohibition to work on the Sabbath (Shabbat) and certain dietary restrictions. *See also* Shabbat.

Palestine *See* British Mandate Palestine.

Pier 21 A major port of entry for immigrants to Canada in Halifax, Nova Scotia. During the years it operated, between 1928 and 1971, approximately one million immigrants passed through Pier 21. The site is now occupied by the Canadian Museum of Immigration at Pier 21.

post-traumatic stress disorder (PTSD) A condition that results from experiencing or witnessing an extremely traumatic event. Symptoms of PTSD can include nightmares and flashbacks, severe anxiety, negative mood, and avoidance of situations and people associated with the traumatic event.

Rosh Hashanah (Hebrew; New Year) The two-day autumn holiday that marks the beginning of the Jewish year and ushers in the High Holidays. It is celebrated with a prayer service and the blowing of the shofar (ram's horn), as well as festive meals that include symbolic foods such as an apple dipped in honey, which symbolizes the desire for a sweet new year.

Salzwedel A concentration camp in Salzwedel, Germany, that was a subcamp of the Neuengamme concentration camp, established in the summer of 1944. The camp held approximately 1,500 female inmates who were used as slave labourers in a munitions factory. In April 1945, women from nearby evacuated camps were brought to Salzwedel, raising the number of inmates to approximately 3,000. The camp was liberated by the US Army on April 14, 1945.

Shabbat (Hebrew; Sabbath) In Judaism, the weekly day of rest beginning Friday at sunset and ending Saturday at nightfall, ushered in by the lighting of candles on Friday evening and the recitation of blessings over wine and challah (egg bread). A day of celebration as well as prayer, it is customary to eat three festive meals, attend synagogue services and refrain from doing any work or travelling.

SS (abbreviation of Schutzstaffel; Defence Corps) The elite police force of the Nazi regime that was responsible for security and for the enforcement of Nazi racial policies, including the implementation of the "Final Solution"—a euphemistic term referring to the Nazis' plan to systematically murder Europe's Jewish population. The SS ran the concentration and death camps and also established the Waffen-SS, its own military division that was independent of the German army.

Star of David (in Hebrew, Magen David) The six-pointed star that is the most recognizable symbol of Judaism. During World War II,

Jews in Nazi-occupied areas were frequently forced to wear a badge or armband with the Star of David on it as an identifying mark of their lesser status and to single them out as targets for persecution.

United Nations (UN) An international organization with 193 member states. It was established in 1945 at the end of World War II to address global issues and promote peace, security and economic development.

War Orphans Project An initiative established in April 1947 by the Canadian Jewish Congress (CJC) to bring orphaned Holocaust survivors under the age of eighteen to Canada. In 1947, the CJC convinced the Canadian government to reissue Privy Council Order 1647—which in 1942 had advocated, too late, for bringing orphans from Vichy France to Canada—thereby allowing 1,000 Jewish children under the age of eighteen to enter Canada. Between 1947 and 1952, 1,123 young Jewish refugees came to Canada.

Yom HaShoah (Hebrew; Holocaust Memorial Day) An annual day of remembrance for Jewish communities around the world to commemorate the six million Jews who were killed in the Holocaust. Yom HaShoah occurs on the anniversary of the Warsaw Ghetto Uprising in the Hebrew calendar, on the 27th day of the month of Nissan, which falls in April or May.

Yom Kippur (Hebrew; Day of Atonement) A solemn day of fasting and repentance that comes eight days after Rosh Hashanah, the Jewish New Year, and marks the end of the High Holidays.

Zionism A movement promoted by the Viennese Jewish journalist Theodor Herzl, who argued in his 1896 book *Der Judenstaat* (*The Jewish State*) that the best way to resolve the problem of antisemitism and persecution of Jews in Europe was to create an independent Jewish state in the historical Jewish homeland of biblical Israel. Early Zionists also promoted the revival of Hebrew as a Jewish national language.

Index

The Azrieli Foundation was established in 1989 to realize and extend the philanthropic vision of David J. Azrieli, C.M., C.Q., M.Arch. The Foundation's mission is to support a wide spectrum of initiatives in education and research. The Azrieli Foundation is an active supporter of programs in the fields of education, the education of architects, scientific and medical research, and the arts.

The staff members dedicated to the Holocaust Survivor Memoirs Program are: Jody Spiegel, Arielle Berger, Catherine Person, Marc-Olivier Cloutier, Carson Phillips, Catherine Aubé, Matt Carrington, Devora Levin, Michelle Sadowski, Elizabeth Banks, Monika Kolanka, Emily Standfield, Candace Alper, Susanne Bachert, Mark Weissfelner, Emily Dychtenberg and Anne Marguet.